Nita Mehta's

INDIAN COOKING with OLIVE OIL

LEONARDO® Olive Oil

SNAB
Excellence in Books

Nita Mehta's

INDIAN COOKING with OLIVE OIL

Most doctors recommend a complete switch over to olive oil during post cardiac problems. Why not switch earlier and prevent problems before they arise?

SNAB
Excellence in Books

The Easiest Change You Can Make

Even with a regular Indian diet, you can prevent heart problems, fight cancer and increase life expectancy

The secret ingredient: olive oil

Olive Oil is universally accepted as a miracle food. Poets have sung about it, doctors have raved about it and chefs cannot do without it. The whole world has switched to Olive Oil for its daily cooking. Why not us?

Because, for some reason, no one took the trouble to educate us! No one told us that there are different grades of Olive Oil for different uses. No one explained to us how exactly Olive Oil's unique properties benefit our health. So, we continue to believe in myths that convinced us Olive Oil wasn't the right oil for Indian homes. It is high time someone busted those myths!

Myth 1: Olive Oil can't be used for Indian cooking.
Fact: Yes, it can! Especially if you use the right grade: Olive Pomace Oil.

We tend to pick up Extra Virgin Olive Oil from the shelves because we've heard it's the best oil. Best flavour, sure, but not best for cooking Indian cuisine! When we tried to cook Indian cuisine with Extra Virgin, we found that the taste changed! Frying in Extra Virgin also presented difficulties.

No one told us that Extra Virgin is a somewhat heavy and viscous oil, when compared to other grades of Olive Oil, and is best suited for raw use in dressings, dips and flavourings.

In fact, it's the humble Olive Pomace Oil that is the cooking grade oil. Pomace oil is used all over Italy, Spain and the Mediterranean for every type of cooking. It is a light oil with neutral taste and flavour. Olive Pomace Oil can be used for all methods, types and varieties of Indian cooking; it neither changes the taste nor presents any difficulties while cooking. Indian cuisine, whether fried, roasted, 'bhunoed' or cooked by any other method, tastes as good with Olive Pomace Oil as with the usual refined oil in your kitchen.

Myth 2: Olive Oil should not be heated and is thus not suitable for frying.
Fact: Olive Pomace Oil is one of the best oils for high-heat cooking and frying!

It's true that Extra Virgin Olive Oil has a low smoking point. Many of its antioxidants are lost when it is heated. The best use of Extra

Virgin is raw, when the full benefits of its flavour and health attributes can be experienced.

Olive Pomace Oil, however, has a smoking point of 238 degrees C, one of the highest amongst culinary oils. Its benefits are especially apparent when frying at between 130 and 238 degrees C. At these temperatures, olive oil forms a crisp, golden crust, making the fried food much more appetizing but without affecting its nutritional value. During the process, the oil hardly penetrates the food, leaving it light and digestible.

What's more, Olive Pomace Oil may be re-used 3-4 times as long as it is filtered carefully after each use through gauze, muslin or a suitable paper filter.

Myth 3: Olive Oil is too expensive.
Fact: No, it isn't, if you use the right grade and use it correctly!

Your doctor may tell you that you can't put a price tag on good health but the one you see on olive oil sure pinches!

Don't be misled by the price tag because, even though Olive Oil costs more than other edible oils, it is economical to use since it is used in 1/3rd the quantity of other edible oils. Since Olive Oil has a high smoking point, it can also be reused 3-4 times.

Used in 1/3rd the quantity and reusable 3 times, the effective cost of Olive Oil is 1/9th its actual price!

Moreover, make sure you use the right grade of Olive Oil for the right purpose. Olive Pomace Oil is the lowest priced Olive Oil - as low as half the price of Extra Virgin - and provides optimum value for money as the best cooking grade oil for Indian cuisine.

And then, there is the greatest FACT of all: Olive Oil is the World's Healthiest Cooking Oil. Prevent Heart Problems, Increase Life Expectancy!

With low saturated "bad" fats and the highest content of mono unsaturated "good" fats amongst all oils, Olive Oil reduces LDL or bad cholesterol and helps prevent heart disease and diabetes. Olive Oil is also packed with anti-oxidants that fight against cancer, reduce the effect of aging and increase life expectancy significantly.

Making olive oil a part of your daily cooking can bring instant and easy wellness to your family's diet.

Leonardo Olive Pomace Oil for Indian cuisine and frying

Leonardo Olive Oil (100% *Pure*) for Western cuisine (eg.Italian) and body massage

Leonardo Extra Virgin Olive Oil and **Leonardo Gold *Premium* Extra Virgin Olive Oil** for salad dressings and dips

Leonardo Olive Oil is available at all leading retailers or order online for free home delivery on www.dalmiaglobal.com

LEONARDO® Olive Oil

Dalmia Continental Pvt. Ltd.
10, Darya Ganj, New Delhi 110002
Tel: (011) 43744900
Email: info@dalmiaglobal.com
Website: www.dalmiaglobal.com

Contents

CURRIES AND DALS 91

RICE AND ROTI 121

DESSERTS 133

Snacks

Broccoli Peanut Kebabs

Roasted crushed peanuts add texture and bite to these broccoli kebabs. A thick sauce of oats cooked in milk is used to bind the mixture. The kebabs are pan-fried to get a crisp brown surface while inside they are deliciously green and moist.

Makes 6-8

200 gms broccoli (1 small flower) - chopped finely along with tender stalks (1½ cups)

1 onion - chopped finely

¼ cup roasted peanuts - crushed coarsely with a rolling pin (*belan*)

1 tbsp Leonardo Olive Pomace Oil

OAT SAUCE

2 tbsp Leonardo Olive Pomace Oil

¼ cup oats

¾ cup milk

½ tsp salt and ¼ tsp pepper, or to taste

1. Break broccoli into florets & wash well. Chop the broccoli florets and the tender stems finely.
2. Heat 1 tbsp Leonardo Olive Pomace Oil in a pan. Add onion and saute for a minute. Add broccoli and 2 pinches of salt and stir on low heat for 2-3 minutes till slightly tender. Remove from heat.
3. Add peanuts to broccoli and keep aside.
4. For the oat sauce, heat 2 tbsp Leonardo Olive Pomace Oil and add the oats. Saute till they start to change colour. Remove from heat and add milk. Mix well and return to heat. Stir on medium heat till thick. Cook till the sauce thickens and starts leaving the sides of the pan.
5. Add salt, pepper and broccoli to the oat mixture. Cook further for 2 minutes on low heat. Remove from heat and cool completely. If in a hurry, refrigerate the mixture so that it becomes firm enough to handle.
6. Make round kebabs, keeping them a little thick. Fry in a pan greased with Leonardo Olive Pomace Oil. Turn sides to brown both sides lightly. Serve.

Vadi Kebabs

The strong flavours of moong dal vadis are combined with paneer, onions, tomatoes, capsicum, garlic and ginger to produce an exotic kebab! Breadcrumbs are used to bind the mixture. On the surface you see a tempting golden colour, and inside you find an explosion of flavour!

Makes 15 pieces

250 gms moong dal vadi
2 tbsp lemon juice
4 tbsp Leonardo Olive Pomace Oil
¾ cup dry bread crumbs - enough to bind
¼ cup chopped coriander
red chilli powder and garam masala to taste

CRUSH TOGETHER

seeds of 4 green cardamoms (*chhoti elaichi*)
2 cloves (*laung*)

OTHER INGREDIENTS

¾ cup grated paneer
¾ tbsp ginger-garlic paste
½ onion - finely chopped
3-4 green chillies - finely chopped
½ tomato - finely chopped
½ of a green capsicum
1 tsp salt or to taste

1. Boil vadi for 3-4 minutes in water. Pat dry on a kitchen towel. Cool. Break into pieces.
2. Grind vadi with all the other ingredients - paneer, ginger garlic, onion, coriander, chillies, tomato and capsicum. Add salt to taste.
3. Remove from grinder and add bread crumbs, lemon juice and 4 tbsp Leonardo Olive Pomace Oil, coriander and freshly ground spices. If the vadis are not spicy, add garam masala and red chilli powder to the kebab mixture.
4. Make small balls and flatten to make kebabs. Cook on a hot pan greased with just 2 tbsp Leonardo Olive Pomace Oil till well browned on both sides. Serve hot.

LEONARDO
Olive Pomace Oil
For Indian Cuisine and Frying
250 ml

Smoked Chicken Chaat

Learn to give a smoked flavor to chicken cubes, as explained in the recipe, then sauté them lightly with garlic. Marinate the veggies and sauté them with carom seeds. Toss everything together, adding pineapple cubes and some zesty spices! Paneer cubes can be used instead of chicken.

Serves 4

SMOKED CHICKEN

3 chicken breasts - cut into ½″ thick strips and then into 1″ pieces or or 300 gms paneer - 1″ pieces

½ tsp each - salt and red chilli flakes, crushed black pepper

1 tbsp Leonardo Olive Pomace Oil

5-6 pieces of coal (get from your press waala)

2 tbsp chopped fresh coriander

OTHER INGREDIENTS

4 tbsp Leonardo Olive Pomace Oil, 1 tsp grated garlic

¼ tsp carom seeds (*ajwain*)

1 onion - cut into 8 pieces

6-8 small mushrooms - remove stalk and keep whole

½ green and ½ red capsicum - cut into 1″ pieces

2 slices of fresh pineapple - cut each slice into 6 pieces

1 tbsp lemon juice, ½ tsp salt, ¼ tsp black salt

½ tsp pepper, ¼ tsp red chilli powder

1 tsp chaat masala, 1 tsp cumin powder (*jeera powder*)

1. Wash chicken. Pat dry. Cut into ½″ strips and then into squares. Rub ½ tsp salt, pepper and red chilli flakes on it. Place a small steel bowl or a *katori* in a kadhai with a lid. Put the chicken around the empty steel *katori*. Place the coal pieces on the naked flame for 5-7 minutes, till they turn grey and red hot at the edges. Put burning coal pieces in the steel *katori*. Pour some Leonardo Olive Pomace Oil on the coal and cover immediately to trap the smoke. Leave covered for 10 minutes for the chicken to acquire a smoky flavour. You can smoke the paneer also in the same way.
2. Marinate onion, capsicums and mushrooms in lemon juice, salt, pepper, chaat masala, cumin powder and crushed garlic. Do not marinate pineapple.
3. To serve, heat 2 tbsp Leonardo Olive Pomace Oil in a pan. Add carom seeds and wait for it to crackle. Add the marinated vegetables and pan fry without stirring much to get that charred, blackened look. Add pineapple and cook for 2-3 minutes.
4. While the veggies are being done, on the other side, heat 2 tbsp Leonardo Olive Pomace Oil in a pan. Add grated garlic and stir. Add smoked chicken. Cook on medium heat, stirring continuously otherwise the chicken will stick to the pan. Fry 3-4 minutes without stirring much till chicken turns whitish and light golden from various sides. Remove chicken from heat when cooked.
5. Mix chicken, veggies, pineapple and coriander. Serve in a platter.

Masala Idli

These idlis are so light because of the addition of yogurt, soda bicarb and soda water. Oats make these idlis trendy but the flavour is traditional.

Serves 12

1 cup semolina (*suji*)

1 cup yogurt
½ tsp soda bi carb (*mitha soda*)
½ cup water
1 tbsp Leonardo Olive Pomace Oil
½ tsp mustard seeds (sarson)
a few curry leaves
1 tsp eno fruit salt

1. Mix semolina, yogurt, water and soda bi-carb.
2. Heat 1 tbsp Leonardo Olive Pomace Oil, add mustard seeds, let them splutter. Add a few curry leaves. Add this to idli batter and mix well. Keep aside for 10 minutes.
3. Heat a big pan with 1" water in it.
4. Add eno fruit salt to idli batter and mix quickly. Pour 2 tbsp batter in lightly greased idli cups of the idli stand.
5. Put idlis in boiling water and steam for 12 minutes on medium heat. Remove pan from heat but let idlis be in steam for 5 minutes. Remove idlis with a wet knife and serve hot.

Bajra & Veggie Bhel

A great health-booster salad using cooked millet, mixed sautéed vegetables and flax seeds, tossed with lemon, vinegar and Leonardo Olive Pomace Oil.

Serves 4

¾ cup millet (*bajra*)

200 gms mix vegetables (bell peppers, cabbage, carrots, cucumber, boiled potato, tomato, onion, mushrooms etc.)
1 tsp flax seeds - roasted
2 tsp lemon juice
½ tsp vinegar
1 tbsp Leonardo Olive Pomace Oil
salt to taste
1 tsp black pepper

1. Dry roast millet for 5-7 minutes.
2. Add about 4 cups water and cook for about 10-15 minutes until millet is soft and cooked.
3. Drain the millet.
4. Saute vegetables together in 1 tbsp Leonardo Olive Pomace Oil for 1-2 minutes.
5. Add the sautéed vegetables to the cooked millet.
6. Add vinegar, lemon juice and black pepper, salt, flax seeds and toss the bhel well. Serve.

TIP: Bajra contains phytochemicals that lower cholesterol. It contains plenty of fiber, iron magnesium, vitamin E and B complex. Magnesium improves the metabolism of the body. Flaxseeds are best plant source of phytoestrogens and Omega 3 fatty acids. It is a complete protein source.

LEONARDO
Olive Pomace Oil
For Indian Cuisine and Frying
Trans-fat Free
Highest MUFA*
Low Saturated Fats

Paneer - Mushroom ke Tinke

Short bamboo skewers laden with colourful cubes of paneer, mushroom, onion, tomato and capsicum, lightly grilled. The secret is in the marinade – sweet, hot and sour, to tantalize your taste buds!

Makes 6-8

7-8 mushrooms, washed & cleaned

150 gms cottage cheese/paneer - cut into 6 pieces
1 onion - cut into chunks and separated
1 large capsicum - deseeded & cut into chunks
2 medium tomatoes - cut into medium pieces and deseeded
1 tsp red chili flakes
½ tsp cumin (*jeera*) powder
½ tsp garam masala powder
½ tsp lemon juice
½ tsp raw mango powder (amchoor)
½ tsp honey
1 tbsp Leonardo Olive Pomace Oil
1¼ tsp salt or to taste

GRIND TO A PASTE

2-3 green chilies - chopped
1 tsp ginger - chopped
4-5 garlic flakes - chopped

1. Grind ginger, garlic and green chillies into a fine paste.
2. In a bowl mix together Leonardo Olive Pomace Oil, prepared paste, red chili flakes, honey, cumin powder, garam masala powder, salt, lemon juice and raw mango powder.
3. Marinate paneer, mushrooms, tomatoes, and capsicum and onion chunks in this mixture for about an hour.
4. Thread them on a wooden stick and cook them directly over gas flame rotating the stick for 5 minutes until evenly cooked. Alternately, put under a hot grill for 7-8 minutes. Serve them with a green chutney dip.

LEONARDO
Olive Pomace Oil

Punjabi Chicken Satay

These flat strips of chicken which cook so quickly are loaded with an orchestra of flavours. A 5-star presentation made in easy steps.

Makes 10-12

2 chicken breasts
a few bamboo skewers

MARINADE

4 tbsp Leonardo Olive Pomace Oil
¼ cup tomato puree
1½ tbsp crushed garlic
2 tsp red chilli-garlic spread
½ tsp each of garam masala, red chilli powder, black pepper
2 tbsp dry fenugreek leaves (*kasoori methi*)
1 tsp sesame seeds
½ tsp salt

PUNJABI MASALA (CRUSH TOGETHER)

1 tsp cumin seeds (*jeera*)
seeds of 1 black cardamom (*elaichi*)
4-5 pepper corns (*saboot kali mirch*)
2-3 cloves (*laung*)
¼ tsp carom seeds (*ajwain*)
1 tsp coriander seeds (*saboot dhania*)

1. Cut the chicken breast horizontally almost till the end and open it up to get a thin, big piece resembling a butterfly shape. Cut chicken into thin strips of 1" width
2. Crush all ingredients of the punjabi masala in a pestle and mortar.
3. Mix all ingredients of the marinade in a bowl. Add the punjabi masala and mix well.
4. Marinate chicken strips in the marinade for about ½ hour. If marinated longer, keep covered in the refrigerator for 1-2 hours or overnight in fridge.
5. Weave chicken strips on a skewer. Flatten them slightly by hitting lightly with a rolling pin.
6. To serve, grease a non stick tawa with Leonardo Olive Pomace Oil. Place all the skewers and cook on medium heat for about 3 minutes, 1½ minutes on each side. Do not overcook.

Ajwaini Murg

Carom seeds (ajwain) bring something new and different in this marinated, sautéed chicken, wrapped in a cream and yogurt coating – finger-licking good!

Serves 4-6

1 chicken (750 gms) - cut into 6-8 pieces, or 8 drumsticks
½ cup yogurt (*dahi*)
2 tsp carom seeds (*ajwain*)
1 tbsp ginger-garlic paste
½ tbsp coarsely crushed red chillies
½ cup thick cream or malai (*milk topping*)
salt to taste
3 tbsp Leonardo Olive Pomace Oil
½ cup chopped fresh coriander

1. Marinate the chicken with yogurt, carom seeds, ginger-garlic paste, red chillies and salt for 30 minutes.
2. Heat Leonardo Olive Pomace Oil in a heavy bottomed pan. Add the chicken pieces leaving behind the marinade.
3. Cook on high heat till the chicken turns brown and all the juices get absorbed. Do not overlap the pieces of chicken while browning.
4. Lower the heat. Add the marinade which is left behind.
5. Add ½ cup of water. Cover and cook on low heat, till the chicken turns tender.
6. Add cream and coriander. Stir fry till the chicken is dry and coated with coriander. Serve hot.

LEONARDO®
Olive Pomace Oil
For Indian Cuisine and Frying
Trans-fat Free
Zero Cholesterol
Highest MUFA*

Quick Corn Chat

Leonardo Olive Oil is added to hot boiled corn – no cooking required. Mix in chopped tomato, onion, green chilli and paneer for a tangy and spicy dish that is also rich in fibre, calcium and protein to give you energy and protect your heart.

Serves 2-3

150 gms (1 cup) corn kernels, frozen or fresh

1 onion - chopped
1 tomato - chopped
1-2 green chillies - chopped
50 gms paneer- grated
½ tsp black salt
½ tsp chaat masala
½ tsp black pepper
salt to taste
1 tbsp Leonardo Olive Oil
1 tsp lemon juice

1. Boil 4 cups water with 1 tsp salt. Add corn and bring to a boil. Remove from heat if using frozen. If using fresh corn available in packets at vegetable vendors, boil for 4-5 minutes till soft. Strain and put in a bowl.
2. Drizzle Leonardo Olive Oil over the hot corn and mix well.
3. Add all the other ingredients along with grated paneer and mix. Garnish with mint and coriander leaves.

Channa Buns

The filling is a blend of chickpeas, spinach, paneer, roasted cumin, amchoor, chilli flakes and other zingy flavours to bring out a hot and sour edge. Stuff into hollowed buns and grill!

Makes 8

8-10 whole wheat burger buns

FILLING

½ cup chick peas (*kabuli channas*) - soak overnight, a pinch of baking soda
2 tbsp chopped fresh coriander
1½ cups shredded spinach
½ cup paneer - crumbled
3 tbsp Leonardo Olive Pomace Oil
1 tsp chopped garlic, 1 tsp chopped ginger
1 onion - chopped finely
½ cup ready made tomato puree
1 green chilli - chopped
1 tsp each - red chilli flakes, coriander powder
1 tsp salt, ½ tsp dry mango powder (*amchoor*)
½ tsp roasted cumin (*bhuna jeera*) powder
½ tsp pepper, ¼ tsp garam masala

1. For the filling, drain chick peas. Add 1½ cups water, a pinch of baking soda and ½ tsp salt and pressure cook to allow one whistle. Reduce heat. Keep on low heat for 20 minutes. Remove from heat and let the pressure drop by itself. Check channas to see that they are well cooked.
2. Heat Leonardo Olive Pomace Oil. Add ginger-garlic and stir for a few seconds. Add onion and cook till golden brown. Add spinach and saute on medium flame for 2 minutes.
3. Add puree and green chilli, dry mango powder, red chilli flakes, coriander powder, salt, roasted cumin powder and pepper. Stir for 2-3 minutes
4. Add chick peas along with the water and coriander. Mash once or twice and stir fry for about 2-3 minutes till masala coats the chick peas.
5. Add paneer. Mix well for 1 minute. Remove from heat. Check taste. Keep aside to cool.
6. Empty the buns by making a hollow in the centre. Brush edges and all around with Leonardo Olive Pomace Oil. Fill with chickpea filling and put under a preheated grill for 6 minutes till crisp and golden at the edges. Serve.

LEONARDO
Olive Pomace Oil

Fish Kebabs

A mouth-watering package of fresh herbs and spices mixed with boneless fish. Add a crisp coating of breadcrumbs and you have a winner!

Makes 15

200 gms boneless fish - roughly chopped
½ onion - chopped
2 green chillies - roughly chopped
1 tsp ginger paste
1 tsp garlic paste
1 tsp salt
1 tsp lemon juice
½ tsp garam masala
2 tbsp chopped fresh coriander
1 tbsp coriander (*dhania*) powder
2 tbsp fresh mint - chopped

OTHER INGREDIENTS

1 egg
1 cup dry crumbs
Leonardo Olive Pomace Oil for frying

1. Mix all the ingredients together in a bowl. Grind them together to make a smooth paste.
2. Add about ½ cup bread crumbs to get a stiff mixture that can be shaped into kebabs.
3. Beat eggs well. Add a pinch of salt and keep aside.
4. Put ½ cup bread crumbs in a flat plate.
5. Make small balls with the fish mixture and flatten them to give them a kebab shape. Make 2″ round kebabs.
6. Dip kebabs first in egg and then coat with bread crumbs. Keep in the fridge to set for 1 hour.
7. Deep fry 3-4 pieces at a time in 5-6 tbsp Leonardo Olive Pomace Oil till golden brown on both sides. Serve hot with any dip.

Rajasthani Paneer Chilla

The batter for this amazing pancake is made from ground yellow moong dal. Paneer fingers are lightly sautéed to make the filling. The step-by-step instructions will make it easy for you to produce this elegant masterpiece.

Makes 10-12

BATTER

1 cup yellow moong dal

2 green chillies - chopped very finely

1 tsp cumin seeds (*jeera*), 3-4 flakes garlic - chopped

ADD LATER

1 tsp salt

2 tbsp very finely chopped fresh coriander

1 tbsp gram flour (*besan*)

FILLING

150-200 gms paneer - cut into 2½"-3" long fingers

2 tbsp finely chopped coriander leaves

2 tbsp Leonardo Olive Pomace Oil

½ tsp garam masala

¼-½ tsp salt, ½ tsp degi mirch or red chilli powder

1. Soak dal for 3-4 hours only, not overnight.
2. Strain. Grind along with green chillies, cumin seeds and 3-4 flakes garlic to a smooth paste. Add salt and coriander. Beat well to make it light, adding about 1 cup water to get a batter of a pouring consistency. Keep aside.
3. Prepare the paneer filling by heating 2 tbsp Leonardo Olive Pomace Oil in a non-stick pan. Add ¼-½ tsp salt, garam masala and red chilli powder. Remove from heat. Add paneer pieces and coriander. Mix paneer with the Leonardo Olive Pomace Oil. Return to heat, saute for a few seconds. Keep aside covered.
4. Mix gram flour with the batter and beat well. Add 1-2 tbsp water if the batter appears thick. Check salt.
5. To make the chilla, heat a non stick griddle (*tawa*), lower the heat, spread 1 tsp Leonardo Olive Pomace Oil with a brush in the centre. With a small *kadchhi* put moong dal batter on the tawa. If using a big *kadchhi*, pour only half *kadchhi* of batter.
6. Spread the batter into a thin round pancake. Let it cook for 2 minutes on low heat till the edges turn brown.
7. Put some Leonardo Olive Pomace Oil on and around the pancake and turn it with the help of a flat spoon. When cooked, turn pancake and place 2 paneer slices to get a long piece. Roll up the pancake with the paneer inside. Serve hot with chutney.

Mustard Jhinga

Prawn-lovers will drool over this one-step-to-success recipe – simply marinate, then bake! The right spice and the right method gets you the right results.

Makes 10

10 prawns - deveined, shelled, wash and pat dry

MARINADE

¾ cup yogurt - hang for 60 minutes to drain out liquid
1½ tsp yellow mustard seed (*rai*) powder
juice of 1 lemon
½ tsp salt to taste
½ tsp red chilli powder
½ tsp black pepper
1 tbsp Leonardo Olive Pomace Oil

1. Mix well all the ingredients of the marinade.
2. Add prawns, mix well and keep it for ½ hour.
3. Place on a wire rack covered with foil. Arrange the prawns on it. Cover with foil again and seal the ends to form a packet. The prawns remain juicy if well packed in foil.
4. Preheat oven at 160°C & place the prawns in foil in the hot oven for 10 minutes or till done.

Sindhi Tikki

Boiled potatoes and breadcrumbs shape these tikkis which hide a treasure inside – minty, tangy, munchy channa dal

Makes 6-8 tikkis

½ kg potatoes - boiled
3-4 bread slices
1 tsp salt
Leonardo Olive Pomace Oil for frying

FILLING

4 tbsp bengal gram (*channa dal*)
½ tsp salt
2-3 green chillies - chopped
1 tbsp green coriander - chopped
2 tsp mint leaves - chopped
1 tsp red chilli powder
1 tsp dry mango powder (*amchoor*)

1. Mash the boiled potatoes well till smooth.
2. Dip the bread slices in water for a second and squeeze out all the water. Add to the mashed potatoes. Add 1 tsp salt and mix well. Keep aside.
3. For the filling, wash dal well, place in a pressure cooker with ½ tsp salt and ½ cup water and give one whistle. Reduce flame and cook for another 10 minutes. Remove from heat and let the pressure drop by itself. Drain dal and place in a bowl.
4. Add coriander, mint leaves, green chillies and powdered masalas to the boiled dal and mix well.
5. Take a handful of mashed potatoes and flatten it with your palms. Put the stuffing of dal in it and close it properly from all sides, give it a shape of a round tikki.
6. Heat Leonardo Olive Pomace Oil in a kadhai and deep fry the tikkis for 2-3 minutes on medium flame till golden brown. Remove from Leonardo Olive Pomace Oil and serve hot.

TIP: To save time and fuel, you can put dal with ½ cup water in a steel bowl and arrange it with potatoes in a cooker with enough water and boil both together.

Cucumber Rolls

These delicate and refreshing rolls enclose cheese, olives and jalapenos. Serve cold on a hot day to make your guests feel calm and relaxed!

Serves 8-10

1 thick large green cucumber
2 tsp sweet mango chutney, available ready made
3-4 cheese slices
8-10 jalapeno slices or 2-3 gherkins, sliced
20 sliced black olives
a few tooth picks

MARINADE

1 tbsp Leonardo Olive Oil
2 pinches of salt and pepper

1. Peel cucumber with a peeler from all 4 sides, leaving the centre seedy part to get 18-20 long strips with a green peel on the edges.
2. Place in a flat dish. Sprinkle all the ingredients of the marinade and mix well. Keep aside for 15 minutes.
3. Place a cucumber peel on a flat surface or a chopping board. Place another peel slightly over laping it lengthwise to get a broader strip.
4. Spread just about 1/8 tsp mango chutney on the slices. (The rolls should not taste sweet).
5. Cut a cheese slice into 3 pieces. Place one piece over the cucumber slices.
6. At the end of the strip, place a big jalapeno or gherkin slice.
7. Roll the cucumber strip and secure with a tooth pick with an olive slice inserted in it.
8. Place on a serving platter and loosely cover with a wrap and refrigerate till serving time.

Chicken Tikka

Everyone makes chicken tikka but yours will be the best because these tikkas get their power from two separate marinades: the first one is based in lemon juice and the second one in yogurt.

Serves 6

500 gms boneless chicken - cut into 1½" pieces
some chaat masala and lemon juice to sprinkle

1st MARINADE

2 tbsp vinegar or lemon juice
1½ tsp degi mirch, ½ tsp black pepper
½ tsp salt, 2 tsp ginger-garlic paste

2nd MARINADE

¾ cup yogurt (*dahi*) - hang in a muslin cloth for 1-2 hours
2 tsp Leonardo Olive Pomace Oil
2 tbsp thick malai or cream, 2 tbsp cornflour
2 tsp ginger-garlic paste
1 tbsp tandoori masala, 1 tbsp dry fenugreek leaves (*kasoori Methi*)
¼ tsp black salt, ½ tsp chaat masala
½ tsp garam masala powder, ½ tsp red chilli powder, 1 tsp salt, or to taste
2-3 drops of red colour

BASTING

2 tbsp Leonardo Olive Pomace Oil

1. Wash the chicken pieces. Cut chicken into 1½" pieces. Pat dry on a towel.
2. Marinate the pieces in the 1st marinade for ½ hour.
3. Transfer the hung yogurt to a flat bowl. Beat till smooth. Add all ingredients of 2nd marinade to yogurt. Beat well to get a smooth marinade.
4. Remove the chicken pieces from the 1st marinade. Add to 2nd marinade. Keep aside in the fridge for at least 3-4 hours or for overnight to allow it to absorb the flavourings of the marinade.
5. Heat an electric oven at 200°C or a gas tandoor on gas on moderate flame. Cover the wire rack or grill rack with aluminium foil. Grease foil with Leonardo Olive Pomace Oil, so that the pieces do not stick to it after getting cooked. Place the well coated chicken pieces on it. If you like you can add some onions and capsicum to the second marinade and skewer the chicken and vegetables on bamboo or metal skewers.
6. Roast for 20 minutes till the coating turns a little dry. Baste with melted butter. Roast again for 5 minutes. If the tikkas are cooked and are still not brownish, you can put them under a grill for 2-3 minutes to acquire a tandoori look. Remove from oven. Sprinkle some chaat masala and lemon juice. Serve hot.

Tomatoes with Crusty Mushrooms

Tomato cups are filled with oats and chopped mushrooms. They are baked to make this beautiful presentation that is both juicy red and crusty brown – pure delight in every bite!

Serves 5-6

4 large tomatoes
½ cup oats - dry roasted light golden
2 tbsp Leonardo Olive Pomace Oil
5-6 gms mushrooms - chopped (1 cup)
8-10 flakes garlic - finely chopped (2 tbsp)
2 tbsp chopped fresh coriander
½ tsp salt and ¼ tsp freshly ground pepper, or to taste
2 tbsp Leonardo Olive Pomace Oil

1. Cut tomatoes in half and scoop out the pulp. Sprinkle salt and pepper in side the tomatoes and rub well to season them. Chop the pulp of 2 tomatoes and keep aside.
2. Dry roast oats in a non stick pan light golden. Keep aside.
3. Heat Leonardo Olive Pomace Oil in a non stick pan. Add garlic and mushrooms and stir till mushrooms turn dry and golden. Add oats and seasoning. Stir for 2 minutes. Add pulp of 2 tomatoes and mix.
4. Place the tomatoes cut side up, close together in a single layer in a small, shallow baking dish, so that the tomatoes fit snugly. Stuff the tomatoes with the mushroom-oat filling.
5. Drizzle with Leonardo Olive Pomace Oil.
6. Bake in a moderately hot oven at 200°C for about 12-15 minutes until crust is golden and tomatoes are soft. The tomatoes should slightly disintegrate under the crust.
7. To serve, heat in a microwave till tomatoes turn really soft. Garnish with a coriander leaf and serve at once.

Chicken Kaathi Rolls

These rolls are extra-special for several reasons: the roti dough has boiled potato in it; the chicken pieces are simmered till they fully absorb the highly flavoured, onion-tomato gravy; and they are made with your love for perfection!

Serves 5-6

DOUGH FOR ROTIS

250 gms (2½ cups) plain flour (*maida*)

2 potatoes - boiled and grated

2 tbsp Leonardo Olive Pomace Oil

1 tsp salt or to taste

FILLING

500 gms boneless chicken - cut into ½" pieces

¾ tsp black cumin (*shah jeera*)

1 large tomato - chopped

1 tbsp ginger juliennes, 2 green chillies - cut into thin long slices

1 tsp salt, or to taste

1 tsp red chilli powder, ½ tsp garam masala

1 tsp lemon juice

2 eggs - beaten

2 onions - thinly sliced & mixed with some hari pudina chutney

GRIND TO A PASTE

1 large onion, 1" piece of ginger and 8-10 flakes of garlic

1. For the dough, sift plain flour. Add grated potato, Leonardo Olive Pomace Oil & salt. Mix well. Knead into a firm dough of rolling consistency with some water. Keep aside covered.
2. For the filling, heat 3 tbsp Leonardo Olive Pomace Oil. Add black cumin and wait till it changes colour. Add onion paste and cook till light brown. Add chopped tomato and cook till tomato turns soft. Add salt, garam masala, red chilli powder Add chicken. Add green chilli and ginger juliennes. Cover and cook on low flame for about 5-7 minutes till chicken turns tender and dry. Remove from heat. Add lemon juice and keep aside.
3. Beat eggs and add a pinch of salt and pepper. Keep aside.
4. Make chappatis out of the prepared dough by cooking the rotis lightly on both sides on the tawa. Keep rotis in a casserole, to keep soft.
5. At serving time, heat tawa. Add 1 tsp Leonardo Olive Pomace Oil and fry the chappati on one side only. Do not turn. Pour 2 tbsp of beaten egg on the chappati and flip (turn) the roti to cook the egg. Remove from tawa, keeping the egg coated side up.
6. Sprinkle 1 tsp lemon juice on the egg coated side of the roti. Arrange chicken filling on one end of the roti. Sprinkle some onions on the filling and roll the roti forward tightly to form the Kaathi Roti. Serve hot.

Instant Khaman Dhokla

An 'instant' recipe is such a relief on a busy day. Make dhokla with gram flour (besan) and Eno Fruit Salt. Buy sachets of Eno rather than a bottle. Enjoy the traditional look and taste of this wholesome family favourite.

Serves 6

1½ cups gram flour (*besan*)
¾ cup water
1 tsp sugar, ¼ tsp turmeric powder (*haldi*)
1 tsp salt, 1 tsp green chilli paste, 1 tsp ginger paste
¼ tsp soda-bi-carb (*mitha soda*)
1 tbsp Leonardo Olive Pomace Oil
1½ tbsp eno fruit salt (2 sachet)
2 tsp lemon juice

TEMPERING

2 tbsp Leonardo Olive Pomace Oil
1 tsp mustard seeds (*rai*)
2-3 green chillies - slit into 2 long pieces
1¼ cups water
2 tsp sugar
¼ cup white vinegar

1. Sift gramflour through fine sieve to make it light and free of any lumps.
2. Mix gramflour, sugar, turmeric powder, salt, chilli-ginger paste, soda, Leonardo Olive Pomace Oil and water to a smooth batter. Keep aside for 10-15 minutes.
3. Put 2-3 cups water in a big pan and place a ring (a loose bottom cake tin without the base works well) in it. Keep it for boiling.
4. Grease a 5-6" square cake tin with Leonardo Olive Pomace Oil.
5. Add eno fruit salt to the above batter & pour lemon juice over it. Beat well for a few seconds.
6. Immediately pour this frothy mixture in the greased tin and tap lightly to level it.
7. Place the dhokla tin on the ring. Cover the pan and steam for 12-13 minutes on medium heat, till a knife inserted in the dhokla comes out clean. Remove pan from heat and leave the dhokla covered in it for 5 minutes in steam. Cool and cut into pieces. Carefully remove the pieces and arrange on the platter.
8. To temper, heat Leonardo Olive Pomace Oil, and mustard. As it splutters, add green chillies. Add water and sugar. Bring to a boil. Remove from heat and add vinegar. Spoon the tempering on the dhokla, giving it time to absorb it. Sprinkle chopped coriander. Serve after a while so that the water gets absorbed and the dhokla turns soft.

Crispy Pan Fried Fish

The marinade for the fish pieces has carom seeds while the crusty topping has sesame seeds – you can't go wrong with this partnership!

Serves 2

200 gms boneless fish (basa fish or sole) - cut into 1½" size pieces & ½" thick (4 pieces)

1-2 tbsp cornflour to dust

Leonrdo Olive Pomace Oil for frying

MARINADE

2 tbsp Leonardo Olive Pomace Oil

1 tbsp lemon juice

1 tsp crushed garlic

½ tsp carom seeds

½ tsp salt

¼ tsp pepper

CRISPY TOPPING

1½ tbsp flour (*maida*)

1½ tbsp cornflour

1 egg

a pinch of salt and pepper

3 slices white bread - grind to fresh crumbs in a mixer (1½ cups)

1½ tbsp sesame seeds (*til*)

1. Dust fish with cornflour to absorb excess moisture and keep aside.
2. Mix all ingredients of marinade, add fish pieces to it. Turn side to coat nicely. Leave for ½ hour.
3. For topping, mix cornflour and flour with egg. Add a few tsp water if needed to get a coating batter. Add a pinch of salt and pepper. Keep aside.
4. Mix bread crumbs with sesame seeds.
5. Dip marinated fish in egg batter and press over fresh bread crumbs mixed with sesame seeds to coat. Pan fry fish in 3-4 tbsp Leonardo Olive Pomace Oil and serve.

Zucchini Oat Crunch

Zucchini pieces are hollowed out, marinated, then filled with an exciting blend of oats, onions and carrots. Serve them hot from the oven to delight your guests.

Makes 8-10

1 thick, big, (500 gms) zucchini

MARINADE

½ tbsp garlic
½ tsp salt
2 tsp vinegar
1 tbsp Leonardo Olive Pomace Oil

FILLING

1 tbsp Leonardo Olive Pomace Oil
½ cup oats
4 tbsp finely chopped carrots
2 tbsp finely chopped onions
1 cup milk
½ tsp garam masala
¾ tsp salt
½ tsp pepper
2 tbsp chopped fresh coriander

1. Cut zucchini into 1½″ thick, pieces, about 8-10 pieces. Scoop out each piece carefully with a melon baller keeping the base intact. Chop the scooped zucchini and keep aside.
2. Mix all ingredients of the marinade. Brush all the zucchini pieces, inside and outside with the garlic & Leonardo Olive Pomace Oil marinade. Keep aside to marinate for 15-20 minutes.
3. Heat 1 tbsp Leonardo Olive Pomace Oil, add onions and saute till soft. Add oats and saute for 2 minutes till light golden. Add milk and stir till thick. Add the chopped carrots and scooped and chopped zucchini. Add garam masala, salt and pepper. Stir for 1-2 minutes. Stir in coriander leaves.
4. Fill the marinated zucchini with the filling nicely.
5. Keep the stuffed zucchini on the greased wire rack of the oven and bake in preheated oven at 200°C for 20-25 minutes or till soft.

Main Course Dry Dishes

Masala Lamb Chops

To make the chops super tender, pound the meat lightly, marinate for a couple of hours in a yogurt based marinade, and pressure cook them. First they absorb the flavours of the marinade, then they get more flavouring by absorbing the onion-ginger-garlic gravy in which they are simmered – expect superb results!

Serves 4-5

MARINATE TOGETHER

10 lamb chops (500 gms)
1 cup yogurt (*dahi*)
1 onion - chopped
1 tbsp garlic - crushed
1 tsp ginger paste
2 tbsp Leonardo Olive Pomace Oil
1 tsp red chilli powder, 2 tsp coriander (*dhania*) powder, 1 tsp salt, 1 tsp cumin (*jeera*) powder

CRUSH TOGETHER

1" cinnamon stick (*dalchini*), 1 tsp fennel seeds (*saunf*)
seeds of 2-3 green cardamom (*chhoti elaichi*)
½ tsp peppercorns (*saboot kali mirch*)

MASALA

2 tbsp Leonardo Olive Pomace Oil,1 bay leaf (*tej patta*)
1 onion - grated, 2 green chillies - chopped finely
1 tsp ginger-garlic paste
2 tbsp chopped fresh coriander, ¼ tsp salt
¼ tsp red chilli powder, ½ tsp garam masala
½ tsp cumin (*jeera*) powder, 1 tsp coriander (*dhania*) powder

1. Wash the chops and gently beat the meat on the chops with a mallet or rolling pin to break the fibres and make the end broad with a nice shape. (You can make your meat waala do it for you when you are buying the chops.)
2. Crush the spices - cinnamon, fennel, seeds of green cardamoms and peppercorns in a pestle and motor.
3. Marinate the chops in the marinade ingredients. Also add the crushed spices and mix well. Keep aside for 2-3 hours to let the flavours penetrate.
4. Put the marinated chops along with all the ingredients in a pressure cooker. Pressure cook to give 2 whistles and keep on low heat for 1 minute. Remove from heat. Cool and open the lid. If there is a little liquid, dry it on high flame, but do not dry too much.
5. Heat Leonardo Olive Pomace Oil in a kadhai. Lower the heat. Add bay leaf and onions and saute till golden. Add green chillies and ginger-garlic paste and stir. Mix coriander powder, salt, red chilli powder, cumin powder and garam masala in 2 tbsp water and add to the masala. Add 2 tbsp chopped fresh coriander.
6. Add chops and stir well for 2-3 minutes till masala coats the chops. Serve hot.

Murg Kali Mirch

Chicken pieces are carefully browned in Leonardo Olive Pomace Oil with just a few ingredients to create a simple, satisfying taste for a main course dish that can also be served as an appetizer. Or, you can take it to another level by pouring makhani gravy into the ready dish to make a richer version.

Serves 5-6

1 chicken (800 gms) - cut into 12 pieces
6-7 tbsp Leonardo Olive Pomace Oil
2 tbsp grated ginger
1 tsp salt
1¼ tsp freshly ground pepper
1 tbsp lemon juice (adjust to taste)
some chopped fresh coriander
4-5 peppercorns (*saboot kali mirch*) - coarsely powdered

1. Wash and pat dry pieces of chicken. Cut slits or incisions in all the pieces so that they absorb the flavours well.
2. Heat Leonardo Olive Pomace Oil on medium flame. Add grated ginger. Fry on medium heat till slightly brown.
3. Add chicken, salt and pepper and fry for about 5 minutes, till chicken changes colour.
4. Lower heat, cover and let it cook for about 15 minutes or till chicken is tender.
5. Increase heat, add lemon juice and cook till dry.
6. Sprinkle coarsely pounded pepper and fresh coriander and mix well. Serve hot.

Amrud ki Subzi

An unusual dish of curried guavas! The yogurt-based sweet and tangy sauce does not overwhelm the cubes of fruit that are simmered in it.

Serves 4

5-6 medium sized guavas (semi ripe)
1 tomato - chopped
¾ cup yogurt
1 tbsp coriander (*dhania*) powder
1/3 tsp red chilli powder
½ tsp turmeric (*haldi*) powder
4 tbsp Leonardo Olive Pomace Oil
4 green chillies
1 tsp fennel seeds (*saunf*)
1 tsp cumin seeds (jeera)
a pinch asafoetida (*hing*)
½ tsp salt, or to taste
1/3 tsp garam masala powder
1 tsp dry mango powder (*amchoor*)
¼ cup sugar
1½ tbsp lemon juice

1. Wash, deseed and cut guavas into small pieces.
2. Whisk yogurt with the powdered spices except garam masala.
3. Heat Leonardo Olive Pomace Oil, add chopped green chillies, cumin seeds, fennel seeds followed by asafoetida and stir.
4. Reduce heat. Add whisked yogurt, stirring continuously till Leonardo Olive Pomace Oil separates.
5. Add chopped tomatoes and salt and stir again till fat separates. Add ¾ cup water and let it boil Add guava pieces and let the gravy boil.
6. Lower the heat, cover and cook for 4-5 minutes, stirring occasionally.
7. When the guavas are cooked, add garam masala powder and cook for 3-4 minutes more.
8. Sprinkle sugar and stir for a minute till sugar dissolves. Add lemon juice and mix well. Remove from heat. Serve hot.

Boote ka Keema

A bowl of keema (well-sauteed minced meat) is an ever popular family favourite. Vegetables such as potatoes or peas can be added, but here the unusual choice is to add green gram (boot). This is available for such a short season that its appearance in the market causes great excitement – which you can feel in the dish!

Serves 4

250 gms mutton mince (*keema*)
250 gms green grams (*boote or chholia*)
3 onions - thinly sliced
1 tsp ginger paste
1 tsp garlic paste
¼ tsp turmeric (*haldi*) powder
1 tsp red chilli powder
1 tsp salt or to taste
3 green chillies - finely chopped
¼ cup chopped fresh coriander - chopped
10 fresh mint leaves - chopped
2 tbsp lemon juice
4-5 tbsp Leonardo Olive Pomace Oil

1. Heat Leonardo Olive Pomace Oil in a kadhai. Add onions and stir till golden brown.
2. Add ginger and garlic, cook for 1-2 minutes. Add salt, turmeric, chilli powder, green chillies, coriander and mint.
3. Add mince and fry for about 7-8 minutes till the liquid dries up and separates out as granules. Cook the mince nicely, scraping the sides in between.
4. Add the green gram and ½ tsp salt. Mix well for a minute. Add ½ cup water and cook uncovered for 10-15 minutes on medium flame until mutton is tender.
5. Continue cooking till the excess water dries up. Remove from heat. Squeeze in the lemon juice and serve hot.

Makai Mirch

The sharp contrast of green hot chillies and creamy yellow sweet corn wakes up all the senses. With these clear instructions you can always achieve perfect results and bow to the applause!

Makes 10

10 big, thick dark green chillies with stem (250 gms)

MARINADE

3 tbsp lemon juice, 3 tbsp white vinegar
½ tsp garlic paste
½ tsp salt, ¼ tsp pepper, ½ tsp sugar

STUFFING

½ tin cream style sweet corn (1 cup)
2 tbsp Leonardo Olive Pomace Oil
1 onion - chopped finely
½ tsp crushed garlic
1 green chilli - chopped finely
1 tsp tomato ketchup
½ tsp salt
¼ tsp pepper
1 tsp white vinegar, ¼ tsp white pepper
1 cheese cube - diced into tiny pieces

1. Cut a slit lengthwise in each chilli, leaving the edges intact to hold the filling well. Scoop out the seeds with the help of a knife.
2. Mix all the ingredients of the marinade in a bowl. Put 1 tbsp of marinade in each, shake it well and remove the marinade to the bowl to reuse it. Similarly do with all chillies. Leave aside for ½ hour.
3. For the stuffing, heat Leonardo Olive Pomace Oil in a pan. Add onion and cook till it turns golden.
4. Add garlic and green chilli. Stir.
5. Add cream style corn. Cook for 1-2 minutes.
6. Add ketchup, salt, pepper and vinegar. Cook for 2-3 minutes till dry.
7. Stuff the chillies with this filling. They should be stuffed well but not to bursting point. Cover with a wrap and refrigerate till serving time.
8. To serve, cook in a pan with 2-3 tbsp Leonardo Olive Pomace Oil. Keep the chillies spread out while cooking. Turn when it turns brownish from the bottom. When both sides get lightly browned, cover and cook on low heat for 3-4 minutes till soft.

Kadhai Murg

The appetizing red colour, the signature of this dish, comes from the generous use of tomatoes and tomato puree in the moist coating sauce. Its strength comes from fenugreek seeds and toasted, crushed coriander seeds. In the end, when the chicken is tender, fresh ingredients are lightly stirred in to give an extra zing – capsicum slices and ginger juliennes.

Serves 4-6

1 medium sized (800 gms) chicken - cut into 12 pieces
6-7 tbsp Leonardo Olive Pomace Oil
1 tbsp coriander seeds (*saboot dhania*), 3 whole, dry red chillies
½ tsp fenugreek seeds (*methi dana*)
3 large onions - cut into slices
15-20 flakes garlic - crushed & chopped, 1" pieces of ginger - crushed to a paste (1 tbsp)
4 large tomatoes - chopped, ½ cup ready-made tomato puree or ¾ cup homemade puree
1 tsp red chilli powder, 1 tsp coriander (*dhania*) powder
2 tsp salt, or to taste, ¼ tsp dry mango powder (*amchoor*), ½ tsp garam masala
½ cup chopped fresh coriander, 1 capsicum - cut into slices
1" piece ginger - cut into match sticks, 1-2 green chillies - cut into long slices

1. Put coriander seeds on a tawa. Keep on heat and roast lightly till it just starts to change colour. Do not make them brown. Remove from heat. Crush the coriander seeds on a rolling board and pin to split the seeds. Keep red chillies whole. Keep aside.
2. Heat Leonardo Olive Pomace Oil in a kadhai. Reduce heat. Add fenugreek seeds and dry, whole red chillies and stir for a few seconds till fenugreek seeds turns golden.
3. Add onion and cook on medium heat till light brown.
4. Add garlic and stir for 1 minute. Add ginger paste.
5. Add the crushed coriander seeds, red chilli powder and coriander powder.
6. Add chopped tomatoes. Cook for 4-5 minutes. Add tomato puree.
7. Add salt, dry mango powder and garam masala. Stir for 2-3 minutes.
8. Add chicken and bhuno for 6-8 minutes on medium high flame, stirring well so that chicken attains a nice golden brown colour. Cover & cook for 15 minutes or till tender, stirring occasionally.
9. Add the coriander, capsicum, ginger match sticks & green chilli slices. Mix well for 2-3 minutes and remove from heat. Serve hot.

Saunfiya Bhindi

8 powdered spices are stuffed into ladyfingers and 3 whole spices are sautéed with them, making this not just any dish but a great work of culinary skill created with love and care.

Serves 4

300 gms lady fingers (*bhindi*)
4 tbsp gram flour (*besan*)
4 tsp cumin powder (jeera powder)
2 tsp coriander (*dhania*) powder
2 tsp fennel (*saunf*) - crushed to a powder
2 tsp dry mango powder (*amchoor*)
1½ tsp garam masala
1½ tsp red chilli powder
1½ tsp turmeric powder
1½ tsp salt, or to taste
4 tbsp Leonardo Olive Pomace Oil
½ tsp fennel (*saunf*)
1 tsp nigella seeds (*kalaunji*)
1 tsp cumin seeds (*jeera*)
2 green chillies - whole

1. Wash, cut the head end of lady fingers, keeping the pointed end as it is. Make a slit in each lady finger.
2. In a mixing bowl put gram flour, red chilli powder, cumin powder, coriander powder, powdered fennel, dry mango powder, garam masala, turmeric powder, salt to taste and 1 tbsp Leonardo Olive Pomace Oil and mix well.
3. Stuff this mixture in each lady fingers.
4. Heat 3 tbsp Leonardo Olive Pomace Oil in a pan or a big kadhai, add fennel, nigella seeds and cumin seeds, when fennel starts to change colour, add lady fingers and whole green chillies. Mix well. Cover with a lid and cook on low heat for about 10 minutes till soft.
5. Uncover and cook lady fingers for about 10 minutes till it turns crisp. Serve hot with roti.

Chicken Achaari

The same spices that are used in making hot and sour pickles (achaar) are used in this chicken dish. Yogurt tenderizes the chicken and vinegar brings in the required tartness – an exciting taste to die for!

Serves 4

500 gms chicken - cut into pieces
6 tbsp Leonardo Olive Pomace Oil
3-4 dried red whole chillies
a pinch of asafoetida (*hing*)
2 onions - chopped
2 tbsp ginger-garlic paste
1 tsp red chilli powder
1 tsp turmeric powder
1½ tsp salt, or to taste
1 cup yogurt - whisked
1 tbsp vinegar

CRUSH ROUGHLY

½ tsp onion seeds (*kalaunji*)
1 tsp brown mustard seeds (*rai*)
¼ tsp fenugreek seeds (*methi dana*)
3-4 cloves (*laung*)
1 tsp cumin seeds (*jeera*)

1. Crush onion seeds, mustard seeds, fenugreek seeds, cloves and cumin together lightly.
2. Heat Leonardo Olive Pomace Oil in a pan, add whole red chillies, asafoetida, chopped onions and sauté till onions turn brown.
3. Add ginger-garlic paste and crushed spices and sauté for a minute. Add chicken, red chilli powder, turmeric and salt. Mix well. Sauté for 2 minutes.
4. Whisk yogurt, add to this and mix well. Stir till yogurt dries and Leonardo Olive Pomace Oil separates.
5. When chicken turns tender, add vinegar and mix well. Serve hot with chapatis.

Vegetable Shashlik

The colourful cubed veggies and paneer are soaked in a marinade, threaded on skewers, then pan-fried on low heat. A light tomato-based sauce is drizzled over them – a must-serve dish for every special occasion.

Makes 4 pieces

2″ piece zucchini - cut into 1″ square pieces of 1″ thickness
8 medium florets of broccoli
½ yellow capsicum - cut into 8 pieces
½ red capsicum - cut into 8 pieces
100 gms paneer - cut into 8 pieces (1″ pieces of ¾ ″ thickness) or 8 mushrooms
2″ piece zucchini - cut into 1″ square pieces of 1″ thickness, optional
8 medium wooden skewers

MARINADE

2 tbsp Leonardo Olive Pomace Oil
3 tsp lemon juice, 4 tsp ginger-garlic paste, ½ tsp salt, ½ tsp pepper

SAUCE

2 tbsp Leonardo Olive Pomace Oil
1 small onion - finely chopped
½ cup ready made tomato puree
1 tbsp flour (*maida*)
¼ tsp pepper to taste, ½ tsp garam masala
1 tsp tomato sauce
½ tsp salt
1 tbsp very finely chopped fresh coriander

1. Boil 3 cups water with 1 tsp salt and 1 tsp sugar. Add broccoli and bring to a good boil. Remove from heat and let it be in hot water for 1 minute. Strain and pat dry on a kitchen towel.
2. Place blanched broccoli and all other raw veggies in a plate and sprinkle the marinade ingredients. Mix well. Lightly mix in the paneer. Rub lightly and turn side to coat. Keep aside for 10-15 minutes.
3. For the sauce, heat Leonardo Olive Pomace Oil. Add onions and stir till golden. Add flour and stir for 1-2 minutes. Add tomato puree and stir for 2-3 minutes or till Leonardo Olive Pomace Oil separates. Add 1 cup water and bring to a boil stirring constantly. Add the remaining ingredients and simmer on low heat till thick like a sauce.
4. Thread on a wooden skewer, a piece of green capsicum, paneer, then red capsicum facing the paneer, yellow capsicum and then zucchini or another paneer, a green capsicum facing it and finally top with a broccoli floret. Pan fry on low heat on a greased tawa, pressing the veggies lightly. Do not burn the paneer so keep the heat low.
5. To assemble, place skewers in a serving plate. Drizzle some sauce on them. Put some extra sauce in a separate bowl. If needed microwave to heat through. Serve.

Subzi Stir Fry

Veggies are par-boiled till crisp-tender, then they are stir-fried with a spicy yogurt-tomato blend and scented with cinnamon and cardamom.

Serves 4

1 medium potato - cut into 8 pieces
1 carrot - cut into thin round slices
8-10 french beans - cut into 2″ pieces
8-10 pieces cauliflower - cut into medium florets
2 tbsp Leonardo Olive Pomace Oil
1 bay leaf (*tej patta*)
1″ piece cinnamon (*dalchini*)
1 onion - chopped
1 tsp chopped garlic, 1 tsp chopped ginger
2 green chillies - chopped

MIX TOGETHER

4 tbsp yogurt
2 tbsp tomato puree
1 tsp coriander (*dhania*) powder
¼ tsp garam masala powder
½ tsp chilli powder
½ tsp coarsely crushed pepper
¾ tsp salt
seeds of 3 green cardamoms (*chhoti elaichi*) - crushed

1. Boil 4 cups of water. Add 1 tsp of salt. Add potato. Boil for about 10 minutes till tender. Check with a knife. When the potatoes are done, remove from water. Add carrot, beans and cauliflower to the boiling water. Boil for 1 minute. Leave in hot water for 2 minutes till the vegetables turn crisp-tender. Strain and keep aside.
2. Mix together in a cup - yogurt, tomato puree, coriander powder, garam masala, chilli powder, pepper powder, salt and cardamom seeds. Keep aside.
3. Heat Leonardo Olive Pomace Oil in a kadhai, add bay leaf and cinnamon. Stir and add onions. Cook till light pink and add garlic, ginger and green chillies. Cook for ½ minute.
4. Reduce heat. Add the yogurt mixed with spices and stir fry for 1 minute till slightly thick.
5. Add the vegetables, stir on low flame to coat the masala on the vegetables. Mix well, serve hot with chappati.

LEONARDO®
Olive Pomace Oil

Saag Chicken

The spinach-tomato puree is strongly flavoured with dry fenugreek leaves and garam masala. The chicken pieces are rubbed with garlic paste and chilli powder then sautéed and simmered in the puree. This is a bold and beautiful Spinach-Chicken Curry – nothing shy about it!

Serves 4

½ kg chicken with bones - cut into 5-6 pieces

1 tbsp Leonardo Olive Pomace Oil, 1 tbsp ginger garlic paste, ½ tsp salt, ½ tsp red chilli powder

CURRY

600 - 700 gms spinach (*palak*), choose a bundle with smaller leaves

2 tbsp Leonardo Olive Pomace Oil

½ tsp cumin seeds (*jeera*), 2 onions - chopped

1½ tsp minced garlic (5- 6 flakes)

¾ tsp cinnamon (*dalchini*) powder, ¾ tsp garam masala, ¼ tsp red chilli powder

1 tsp coriander (*dhania*) powder, ¼ tsp amchoor, ¾ tsp salt

2 tomatoes - chopped, 1 green chilli - chopped

1 tbsp dry fenugreek leaves (*kasoori methi*)

BAGHAR (TEMPERING)

1 tsp Leonardo Olive Pomace Oil, 1″ piece ginger - cut into thin long pieces (juliennes)

1 green chilli - slit into long pieces, ½ tsp red chilli powder

1. Marinate chicken with Leonardo Olive Pomace Oil, ginger garlic, salt and red chilli powder. Keep aside.
2. Remove stems of spinach leaves and wash well. Chop roughly.
3. Heat 3 tbsp Leonardo Olive Pomace Oil in a kadhai. Add cumin, onions and garlic. Cook till onion turn light brown.
4. Add cinnamon powder, garam masala, red chilli powder, coriander powder, dry mango powder and salt. Stir on low flame for 1 minute.
5. Add chopped tomatoes and dry fenugreek leaves. Cook for 3-4 minutes, till well blended.
6. Add spinach and green chilli. Cook uncovered for 5-7 minutes on low flame. Remove from heat. Cool.
7. Blend the cooled mixture along with 1 cup water, just for a few seconds, to a coarse paste. Do not grind it too finely. Keep aside.
8. Heat Leonardo Olive Pomace Oil in another kadhai, add chicken and bhuno for 5-7 minutes, stirring continuously till chicken is 80% cooked.
9. Add the prepared green paste. Mix well and cook covered on low heat for 4-5 minutes till chicken turns soft. Check salt and remove from heat.
10. Transfer to a serving dish. Heat 1 tbsp Leonardo Olive Pomace Oil. Add ginger and green chilli. Remove from heat. Add red chilli powder and pour Leonardo Olive Pomace Oil on the hot saag. Mix lightly. Serve.

LEONARDO
Olive Pomace Oil
For Indian Cuisine and Frying
250 ml

Vegetable Jalfrezi

In a jalfrezi you will always find that the ingredients are cut in long strips and have a sweet and sour flavor – exactly like this dish which is highlighted with onion seeds (kalonji) and curry leaves.

Serves 4

150 gms paneer - cut into 1" long pieces of finger thicknes
3 tbsp Leonardo Olive Pomace Oil
½ tsp cumin seeds (*jeera*), ¼ tsp onion seeds (*kalaunji*)
15-20 curry leaves roughly torn
1 onion - sliced
2 tsp ginger-garlic paste
8-10 French beans - sliced diagonally into 1" pieces or 8-10 babycorns - each halved lengthwise
1 large carrot - cut diagonally into thin slices
½ of each - green and yellow capsicum - deseed and cut into thin fingers
½ cup boiled peas
1 long, firm tomato - cut into 4, pulp removed and cut into thin long pieces
1 tsp dry fenugreek leaves (*kasoori methi*)

MIX TOGETHER

½ cup tomato puree, 1 tbsp tomato ketchup
½ tsp degi mirch powder, ½ tsp sugar
1 tsp coriander (*dhania*) powder, ¼ tsp dried mango powder (*amchoor*), 1 tsp salt

1. Mix together — tomato puree, tomato ketchup, degi mirch powder, sugar, coriander powder, dry mango powder and salt in a cup. Keep aside.
2. Heat 3 tbsp Leonardo Olive Pomace Oil in a *kadhai*. Add the cumin seeds & onion seeds together. When cumin turns golden, reduce heat & add curry leaves & stir for a few seconds.
3. Add onion and stir till golden. Add ginger-garlic and stir for a minute.
4. Add carrot and beans/babycorns. Saute for 2-3 minutes.
5. Add the tomato puree mixed with dry masalas, dry fenugreek leaves and stir on medium heat for 2 minutes.
6. Add ¼ cup water. Cook on low heat for about 4-5 minutes, till vegetables are cooked but still remain crunchy.
7. Add the capsicums, boiled peas, paneer and tomato slices. Stir till well blended. Add a pinch of sugar if needed. Remove from heat. Serve hot.

Sai Bhaji

This well-known dish has channa dal cooked with spinach and a variety of chopped veggies. The channa dal has a nutty taste and satisfying munch. This yummy, hearty formula will happily feed the hungry crowd!

Serves 4-5

1 bundle (650-700 gms) spinach - washed and chopped
1 cup channa dal - soaked for 10 minutes, salt to taste,
1 onion - chopped
1 tomato - chopped
2 green chillies - chopped
1 cup mixed vegetables (potato, cabbage, carrot) - chopped

TEMPERING

2 tbsp Leonardo Olive Pomace Oil
1 tsp red chilli powder
4 garlic flakes - chopped

1. In a pressure cooker, put channa dal, onion, tomato, green chillies, vegetables and spinach. Add salt and 1 cup water. Pressure cook for 20 minutes. Remove from heat and let the pressure drop. Mash the spinach with a potato masher. Keep aside.
2. In a pan heat 2 tbsp Leonardo Olive Pomace Oil and put garlic, when it turns pink, put red chilli powder. Remove from heat and pour it into the spinach. Serve hot with plain rice and roasted papads.

Baghaare Baingan

This dish made of stuffed brinjals, a star of Hyderabadi cuisine, uses the traditional ingredients of that region – a paste made of roasted onions, coconut, peanuts and poppy seeds, and the deliciously sour and sweet gift of tamarind and jaggery.

Serves 4

250 gm brinjals (small round variety)
2 onions - cut each into 4-6 pieces
2 tsp roughly chopped ginger
1 tbsp chopped garlic
1 tsp coriander seeds
1½ tbsp sesame seeds (*til*)
3 tbsp roasted peanuts
½ tsp cumin seeds (*jeera*), 1 tsp poppy seeds (*khus khus*)
1 " square piece kopra (*dry nariyal*), a pinch fenugreek seeds (*methi dana*)
¼ tsp turmeric (*haldi*) powder, ¾ tsp red chilli powder
½ tsp jaggery (*gur*) or sugar
1 lemon size ball tamarind - soak in 1 cup hot water for 15 minutes, mash and strain
a few curry leaves, 4 tbsp Leonardo Olive Pomace Oil, ½ tsp salt or to taste

1. Wash brinjals. Make cross-slits along the length of the brinjal ensuring that the brinjal is held together at the stem. Rub a pinch of salt inside each brinjal. Keep aside.
2. Roast the onions on a tawa for 5 minutes, till they soften a little & turn slightly golden brown.
3. Dry roast together, on tawa for a minute over medium heat, the coriander seeds, sesame seeds, peanuts, cumin seeds, poppy seeds, kopra and fenugreek seeds till they give out a roasted smell.
4. Grind together the onions, roasted spices, ginger, garlic, salt, turmeric, red chilli powder and jaggery/sugar to a fine paste. Using only about 2-3 tbsp of this paste, stuff the brinjals. Keep stuffed brinjals aside. Add tamarind water to the remaining paste.
5. Heat Leonardo Olive Pomace Oil in a pan, add curry leaves and after a few seconds, add the stuffed brinjals. Shake the pan instead of stirring, to brown the brinjals evenly, for about 10 minutes on low heat.
6. Add the ground spice paste mixed with tamarind water. Cook covered over medium heat for 5-7 minutes. Add ½ cup water and stir occasionally till brinjals get tender and Leonardo Olive Pomace Oil separates. Serve hot.

Palak Aloo

Give an everyday dish like Spinach and Potatoes a gourmet status by cooking them with onions, garlic, ginger, tomatoes, cardamoms and cinnamon. Boiled potatoes reduce cooking time.

Serves 6

500 gms spinach (*paalak*)
2 small potatoes
1 " piece ginger - grated
3 tbsp Leonardo Olive Pomace Oil
2 black cardamoms (*moti elaichi*)
1 " stick cinnamon (*dalchini*)
5-6 flakes garlic - crushed to a rough paste
2 onions - finely chopped (1 cup)
3 tomatoes - chopped (1½ cups)
½ tsp turmeric (*haldi*) powder
1 tsp ground coriander (*dhaniya*) powder
½ tsp red chilli powder
½ tsp garam masala
1 tsp salt, or to taste

1. Wash and peel potatoes. Cut into 1" pieces. Cut away thick stalks of spinach. Chop leaves finely into thin strips or ribbons.
2. Heat Leonardo Olive Pomace Oil. Reduce heat. Add black cardamoms and cinnamon. Wait for a minute. Add garlic and cook till it starts to change colour.
3. Add onions and stir fry till golden. Reduce heat. Add turmeric powder, ground coriander, chilli powder, garam masala and salt. Mix well on low heat for a minute.
4. Add ginger. Stir for a few seconds. Add tomatoes & stir fry for 3-4 minutes till well blended.
5. Add potatoes. Stir fry for 4-5 minutes. Cook covered for 10 minutes, sprinkling a little water occasionally, till the potatoes turn soft.
6. Add spinach. Continue cooking, without covering, for about 10 minutes, till the spinach gets wilted and is well blended with the potatoes.
7. Serve hot with any bread.

Chowgra

A colourful curry of six different vegetables from Hyderabad, creating a range of textures and flavours. Each vegetable is first fried separately and then mixed together and flavoured with aromatic spices.

Serves 6

2 potatoes - cut into ¾" pieces
2 medium carrots - cut into ¼" thick slices
12-15 French beans - cut into 1 ½" pieces
10-12 medium or 1" size florets of cauliflower
2 thin, long brinjals - cut into half lengthwise and then cut diagonally into 1½" pieces
¼ cup frozen or boiled peas, 3 medium size onions - thinly sliced
1 tsp ginger paste, 1 tsp garlic paste
1 tsp salt, ¼ tsp turmeric powder, 1 tsp red chilli powder
1 cup yogurt - whisked till very smooth
Leonardo Olive Pomace Oil for frying

GRIND TOGETHER

2 green cardamoms (*elaichi*), 4 cloves (*laung*), 1 bay leaf (*tej patta*)
¼" piece of cinnamon (*dalchini*), ¼ tsp black cumin (*shah jeera*)

1. Heat Leonardo Olive Pomace Oil in a kadhai. Deep fry potatoes on low medium heat till golden and almost cooked. Remove from Leonardo Olive Pomace Oil. Add cauliflower and fry till light golden, for about 2 minutes.Add brinjals and deep fry till they start changing colour. Add the carrots and fry for just a minute to retain their colour. Similarly fry the beans for just a minute. Set aside.
2. Remove excess Leonardo Olive Pomace Oil from the kadhai, leaving about 4 tbsp Leonardo Olive Pomace Oil. Heat Leonardo Olive Pomace Oil and add onions. Fry for 8-10 minutes till golden brown.
3. Reduce heat. Add ginger and garlic and fry for a minute. Add salt, turmeric and red chilli powder. Sprinkle 2-3 tbsp water and simmer for 2-3 minutes for the spices to blend well.
4. Keeping heat to a minimum, add the fried vegetables and whisked yogurt. Stir and cook at medium-low heat, till the vegetables are fully cooked. Sprinkle a little water while cooking, if required.
5. Add the ground spices and mix well. Serve hot.

Dum ki Phool Gobi

In this recipe cauliflower is cooked in yogurt and spices on very low heat, tightly covered. It gets infused with the magical aromas of whole garam masalas as it becomes tender – this method is known as 'cooking on dum'.

Serves 4

1 medium cauliflower (*gobhi*) (300-350 gms)

1 cup yogurt (*dahi*), 1 tsp salt, ¾ tsp red chilli powder

SABOOT GARAM MASALA

1 black cardamom (*moti elaichi*), 2-3 cloves (*laung*)

1″ stick cinnamon (*dalchini*), 1 bay leaf (*tej patta*), a pinch of mace (*javitri*)

OTHER INGREDIENTS

3 tbsp Leonardo Olive Pomace Oil

2 onions - chopped, 1″ piece ginger - chopped, 2 green chillies - chopped

¼ tsp turmeric (*haldi*) powder, ½ tsp coriander (*dhania*) powder, ¼ tsp red chilli powder

3 tomatoes - chopped, 8-10 ginger juliennes, 2 tbsp chopped fresh coriander

FOR DUM

seeds of 3 green cardamoms (*chhoti elaichi*) - powdered

1 tbsp dry fenugreek leaves (*kasoori methi*) - roasted in a microwave and crushed to a powder

1 tbsp Leonardo Olive Pomace Oil

1. Break cauliflower into medium sized florets along with a little stalk. Wash well. Drain out the water well.
2. Beat yogurt in a bowl. Add salt and red chilli powder
3. Add cauliflower to the yogurt. Mix well and keep aside to marinate.
4. Heat Leonardo Olive Pomace Oil in a pan/kadhai. Reduce flame and add together all the ingredients given under saboot garam masala. Stir for a minute.
5. Add onions & cook till they turn golden. Add ginger & green chillies. Mix well for ½ minute.
6. Add turmeric, coriander and red chilli powder. Stir.
7. Add tomatoes and stir fry till the masala leaves the Leonardo Olive Pomace Oil.
8. Remove the cauliflower pieces from yogurt and keep aside.
9. Add the yogurt gradually to the masala. Cook till the yogurt turns a little dry.
10. Add the cauliflower pieces. Saute the vegetable for 5-7 minutes.
11. Cover and cook on low flame, till the vegetable is just done, for about 10-12 minutes. Sprinkle some water on the lid in between, putting it in the vegetable after a few seconds, if the cauliflower sticks to the bottom. Do not over-cook the cauliflower.
12. Add ginger shreds and fresh coriander. Mix well.
13. Sprinkle green cardamom powder and dry fenugreek leaves, pour some Leonardo Olive Pomace Oil on top. Cover kadhai with a lid tightly and put it on dum on a tawa on low heat for 10 minutes.

Smoked Paneer Hara Pyaz

Lots of green onions add their sweet and gentle taste to paneer and mushrooms, cooked with tomatoes and spices. Learn how to give a smoky flavor to any dish and take it up to a higher level of excellence.

Serves 4

100 gms paneer - cut into 1″ squares, 100 gm mushrooms - halved or cut into 4 pieces
200 gms spring onions
4 tbsp Leonardo Olive Pomace Oil, 6-8 flakes garlic - chopped, 1 tsp chopped ginger
¼ tsp turmeric (*haldi*) powder
2 tomatoes - pureed in a mixer, 2 tomatoes - finely chopped
1 tbsp tomato ketchup, 3 cloves (*laung*) - crushed roughly
2 tsp coriander (*dhania*) powder
1¼ tsp salt, or to taste, ½ tsp red chilli powder
½ tsp garam masala, 1 green chilli - deseeded & chopped
1 tbsp ginger juliennes

TO SMOKE

a piece of coal
½ tsp Leonardo Olive Pomace Oil

1. Cut white bulb of spring onion into rings and cut green part diagonally into ½″ pieces, keep green separate.
2. Boil 3-4 cups water with 1 tsp salt. Add mushrooms and boil for 2 minutes. Remove from water. Keep aside.
3. Heat 4 tbsp Leonardo Olive Pomace Oil in a wide pan. Add garlic and ginger. Saute for 1 minute on low heat. Add the white of onions and stir fry till light brown.
4. Add ¼ tsp turmeric. Stir for 1 minute. Add fresh tomato puree and chopped tomatoes and stir fry for 5-7 minutes, till they turn almost dry.
5. Add tomato ketchup. Stir to mix well. Add crushed cloves. Cook for ½ minute.
6. Reduce heat. Add coriander powder, salt, red chilli powder and garam masala. Cook for 2 minutes on low heat.
7. Add ¼ cup water. Boil. Add the paneer, mushrooms, greens of onions and chopped green chilli. Cook for 1-2 minutes on low heat till well mixed. Mix in the ginger juliennes. Remove from heat.
8. To smoke the vegetables, shift the vegetables to the edges of the pan. Place a steel *katori* in the centre. Heat a piece of coal till it turns grey at the edges. Place the burning coal in the *katori* and pour little Leonardo Olive Pomace Oil on the coal. Immediately cover the pan to trap the smoke. Let vegetables be smoked for about 10 minutes. Uncover and reheat to serve.

Note: If spring onions are not available, use 1 capsicum cut into thin long pieces and 2 small, ordinary onions cut into thin rings.

Curries & Dals

Paneer Pasanda with Mushroom Curry

A light tomato sauce with minced mushrooms is poured into the plate. Slices of paneer are sandwiched with a veggie-cheese filling, then pan-fried, and placed on the sauce to make an elegant presentation.

Makes 4 steaks

300 gms paneer - cut into ¼" thick rectangles of 2"x1½" size

MARINADE

1 tbsp Leonardo Olive Pomace Oil, ¼ tsp salt

½ tsp each of - red chilli flakes, pepper and oregano

FILLING

2 tbsp Leonardo Olive Pomace Oil

1 small onion - chopped finely

½ cup thickly grated carrot

½ cup shredded spinach, ¼ tsp salt and pepper

¼ tsp grated nutmeg (*jaiphal*)

2 tbsp grated cheddar cheese

2-3 tbsp finely grated mozzarella cheese

MUSHROOM CURRY

2 tbsp Leonardo Olive Pomace Oil

3 mushrooms - finely chopped

2 tbsp flour (*maida*)

1 cup hot water

¼ tsp pepper to taste, ½ tsp garam masala, 2 tbsp tomato puree, 1 tsp tomato sauce

1 clove (*laung*) - crushed

1. Cut paneer into slices carefully. Place on a plate. Sprinkle marinade ingredients. Rub lightly and turn to coat the other side also. Keep aside for 10-15 minutes.
2. For filling, heat 2 tbsp Leonardo Olive Pomace Oil, add onion and cook till golden.
3. Add the spinach, cook till dry, add carrot and stir for 2 minutes. Add salt, pepper and nutmeg. Remove from heat. Add cheddar cheese, cool the mixture.
4. Take 1 slice of paneer and spread the filling, sprinkle with mozzarella cheese and cover with another slice. Repeat with other slices to make pasandas. Keep aside.
5. For the curry, heat Leonardo Olive Pomace Oil. Add mushrooms and stir till golden. Add flour and stir for 1-2 minutes. Add tomato puree and stir for 1-2 minutes. Add hot water and bring to a boil stirring constantly. Add the remaining ingredients and simmer on low heat till thick like a sauce.
6. Pan fry the stuffed pasandas in 2-3 tbsp Leonardo Olive Pomace Oil. To serve, pour a little hot curry on a platter, arrange the paneer pasanda and pour the remaining curry.

Channe Jaisalmer Ke

The yogurt-based gravy is thickened by mashing in some of the boiled black gram, channe. The result is a creamy, fragrant highly nutritious dish, everyone's favourite.

Serves 3-4

1 cup black gram (*kale channe*) - soaked overnight
1 cup yogurt (*dahi*)
4 tbsp gram flour (*besan*)
½ tsp turmeric (*haldi*) powder
1 tsp salt, or to taste
2 tbsp Leonardo Olive Pomace Oil
1 tsp cumin seeds (*jeera*)
1 bay leaf (*tej patta*)
2″ cinnamon stick (*dalchini*)
a pinch asafoetida (*hing*)
1 tbsp ginger-garlic paste
2 green chillies - chopped
½ cup finely chopped fresh coriander

TEMPERING

1 tbsp Leonardo Olive Pomace Oil
½ tsp mustard seeds (*sarson*)
2-3 dry red chillies
1 tsp red chilli powder

1. Drain the soaked channas. Add 4½ cups water and ½ tsp salt, pressure cook to give 2 whistles. Keep on low heat for 20 minutes. When pressure drops, mash some of the channas. Keep aside.
2. Mix together gramflour, yogurt, turmeric powder and 1 tsp salt.
3. Heat Leonardo Olive Pomace Oil in a kadhai, put bay leaf, cinnamon and cumin seeds. When it splutters, add asafoetida and green chillies. Stir. Add ginger-garlic paste and stir for a minute.
4. Add the yogurt mixture and stir continuously till it boils.
5. Add the boiled channa along with water and mix well. Simmer covered for 8-10 minutes, add the green coriander. Check salt.
6. In a pan, heat Leonardo Olive Pomace Oil, add mustard seeds, when they start spluttering add whole red chillies Remove from heat. Add red chilli powder and pour on the channas and serve.

Note: Keep the gravy thick if you are serving with roti, likewise keep the gravy watery if serving with rice.

Chicken Chettinad

Chettinad cooking from the South is famous for its fiery curries, like this one. Poppy seeds, cashews, coconut and milk balance the heat and add complex layers of contrasting flavours.

Serves 4-6

1 chicken (700-800 gms) - cut into 12 pieces
5-6 tbsp Leonardo Olive Pomace Oil, 1 large onion - chopped very finely
¼ cup curry leaves (*curry patta*), 3 tomatoes - pureed in a mixer
1 tsp salt, or to taste, ¼ tsp turmeric (*haldi*) powder, ¼ tsp chilli powder, 2-3 tbsp lemon juice
1 tbsp poppy seeds (*khus khus*), read note given below
2 tbsp cashewnuts(*kaju*) - broken pieces, 1 cup milk
2-3" piece ginger, 8-10 flakes garlic

CHETTINAD MASALA

½ cup freshly grated coconut (remove brown skin before grating)
1 tsp coriander seeds (*saboot dhania*), 1 tsp fennel seeds (*saunf*)
½ tsp cumin seeds (*jeera*), 2½ tsp peppercorns (*saboot kali mirch*)
5-6 whole, dry red chillies, 3 green cardamoms (*chhoti elaichi*)
2-3 cloves (*laung*), 1" cinnamon stick (*dalchini*), 1 tbsp Leonardo Olive Pomace Oil

1. Soak poppy seeds and cashewnuts in a little warm water for 10-15 minutes.
2. Heat 1 tbsp Leonardo Olive Pomace Oil in a pan or tawa. Add coconut, coriander seeds, fennel seeds, cumin, peppercorns, dry red chillies, seeds of green cardamoms, cloves and cinnamon to Leonardo Olive Pomace Oil. Stir-fry till fragrant. Remove from heat.
3. Drain poppy seeds and cashews. Grind together the roasted masala with the drained poppy seeds-cashewnuts, ginger and garlic to a smooth paste in a mixer grinder to a very smooth paste with ¼ cup water. Keep aside.
4. Grind tomatoes in a mixer to a smooth puree. Keep aside.
5. Heat Leonardo Olive Pomace Oil in a kadhai and add the chopped onions. Fry till light brown.
6. Add the chicken and cook or bhuno for 10 minutes or till almost cooked.
7. Add the pureed tomatoes, salt, turmeric and chilli powder. Cook till tomatoes are well blended with the masala and Leonardo Olive Pomace Oil separates.
8. Add the ground paste and curry leaves. Saute for 2 minutes.
9. Add lemon juice and 3 cups of water. Cover and cook till chicken is tender, stirring in between. Cook till the masala is thick. Keep aside till serving time.
10. At serving time, add 1 cup milk to the chicken. Keep on low heat, stirring continuously, till it boils. Serve garnished with coriander.

POPPY SEEDS (*Khus-Khus*)
These are very tiny, beige coloured seeds which have a nutty aroma. They are also sprinkled over naan or breads before being cooked in the oven. These should be stored in the fridge as they turn rancid and acquire an off taste when kept in a warm place.

Goan Fish Curry

Pieces of white fish are gently simmered in a curry of coconut milk and tamarind, tempered with mustard seeds and curry leaves, to create the beautiful taste of Goa.

Serves 4

400 gms of any firm white fish - cut into 2″ pieces
4 tbsp Leonardo Olive Pomace Oil
2-3 green chillies - deseeded and sliced
1 tsp red chilli powder
2 tsp coriander (*dhania*) powder
½ tsp garam masala, 1 tsp salt
2 cups thick coconut milk
2 tbsp tamarind (*imli*) pulp, optional
1 cup water

PASTE

1 medium onion
2½″ piece of ginger
8-10 flakes of garlic

TEMPERING (*TADKA*)

2 tbsp Leonardo Olive Pomace Oil
1 tsp black mustard seeds (*sarson*)
8-10 curry leaves (*curry patta*)
3 whole dry red chillies

1. Make a paste of onion, ginger and garlic in a blender.
2. Heat the Leonardo Olive Pomace Oil in a kadhai, add onion paste & green chillies. Cook until onion turns brown.
3. Add red chilli powder, coriander powder, garam masala and salt. Mix. Cook on medium heat until Leonardo Olive Pomace Oil separates. Sprinkle a little water if the masala sticks to the pan.
4. Add tamarind pulp, coconut milk and 1 cup of water. Let it come to a boil. Add fish and cook on low heat for 10-12 minutes or until the fish is cooked. Remove from heat.
5. For the tempering, heat the Leonardo Olive Pomace Oil in a frying pan add all the ingredients. When the seeds start spluttering pour over the hot fish. Serve hot.

Panchmela Dal

A pressure cooker recipe in which five kinds of Lentils combine their taste, texture and colour to create this uncomplicated classic winner of Rajasthan.

Serves 4

4 tbsp yellow moong dal
2 tbsp white urad dal
4 tbsp channa dal
2 tbsp arhar dal
4 tbsp green chhilka moong
1½ tsp salt or to taste
¾ tsp turmeric powder

TEMPERING

2 tbsp Leonardo Olive Pomace Oil
1 tsp cumin seeds (*jeera*)
a pinch of asafoetida (*hing*)
2 tomatoes - finely chopped
1″ piece ginger - cut into juliennes
2 green chillies - each cut into 2 pieces lengthwise
1 tsp red chilli powder
1 tsp coriander powder
½ cup finely chopped fresh coriander

1. Soak the dals together for ½ hour.
2. Pressure cook along with 2½ cups water, salt and turmeric powder for 2 whistles. Remove from heat and let the pressure drop by itself.
3. For tempering, heat Leonardo Olive Pomace Oil in a kadhai, put asafoetida and cumin. When cumin turns golden, add tomatoes. Cook for 3-4 minutes. Add ginger juliennes, green chillies, red chilli powder and coriander powder. Mix well.
4. Pour the dal on the tempering and mix well.
5. Simmer for 2-3 minutes. Add green coriander leaves and mix. Serve with rice or missi roti or baati.

Dahi ke Kofte in Palak-Methi Curry

These light-as-air koftas are made with yogurt, paneer, chopped almonds and a little flour for binding. They float on a curry that has a smooth base of ground onions, tomatoes, pureed spinach and fenugreek leaves.

Serves 4

KOFTA (12 SMALL)

200 gms yogurt - hang for 3-4 hours to drain out water completely,
50 gms paneer - crumbled, 1 tsp chopped almonds
½ tsp salt, ¼ tsp red chilli powder, ¼ tsp garam masala
2 green chillies - chopped, 2 tbsp chopped fresh coriander, 2 tbsp flour (*maida*), or as needed
a pinch of baking powder, a few raisins,
Leonardo Olive Pomace Oil for frying

GRAVY

½ bunch fenugreek (*bundle methi*) (150-200 gms) - separate leaves
1 bunch spinach (*bundle palak*) (500 -600 gms) - separate leaves
1-2 green chillies, 2 tbsp Leonardo Olive Pomace Oil
4 cloves (*laung*), 1" cinnamon, 2 black cardamoms (*moti elaichi*)
2 onions - grind to a paste, 1 tsp garlic paste, 2 tomatoes - blanch and puree
½ tsp salt or to taste, ½ tsp pepper, ¼ tsp white pepper, ¼- ½ cup milk

TEMPERING

1 tbsp Leonardo Olive Pomace Oil, 1 tbsp juliennes of ginger, ¼ tsp degi mirch powder

1. To prepare koftas, mix hung yogurt, paneer, flour, garam masala, red chilli powder and salt. Sprinkle flour, baking powder and almond bits. Mix well. Make a ball and test it by frying. If it is too soft, add 1-2 tsp flour to the mixture. Make balls with greased hands and stuff half of a raisin inside each ball. Refrigerate. Deep fry just 2-3 pieces at a time.
2. To prepare the gravy, boil 6-7 cups water with 1 tsp salt and 1 tsp sugar. Add spinach and boil for 2-3 minutes. Remove from water.
3. Add 1 more tsp salt to boiling water and add fenugreek leaves. Boil for 5-6 minutes. Remove from water.
4. Grind cooled spinach and fenugreek with 2 green chillies to a paste.
5. Heat Leonardo Olive Pomace Oil. Add claves, cinnamon & black cardamoms. When fragrant after a few seconds, add onion paste and stir fry till golden. Add garlic paste. Stir for a minute.
6. Add blanched & pureed tomatoes. Cook till dry & Leonardo Olive Pomace Oil separates.
7. Add green paste and bhuno for 5-7 minutes. Add salt and black pepper.
8. Add 1½ cups water and bring to a boil. Add white pepper. Add milk according to the consistency that you like.
9. To serve, microwave koftas to warm them for 1 minute. Heat curry, adding some water if thick. Transfer to a serving dish. Top with warm koftas.
10. To temper, heat Leonardo Olive Pomace Oil. Add bay leaves and ginger. Stir till it turns golden. Remove from heat and add and degi mirch. Pour the Leonardo Olive Pomace Oil over the palak-methi curry.

Manzil-e-Paneer with Low Cal Makhani Gravy

On the serving platter, make a 'loaf' of golden paneer slices sandwiched with an unusual brinjal-corn filling. Pour the gravy over it. There is no cream or butter in this gravy but it tastes deliciously rich and thick.

Serves 8

400 gms soft paneer - cut into thin slices, a few pinches of red chilli powder, salt, chat masala

FILLING

1 (250-300 gms) round brinjal - roasted and mashed with a knife to get 1-1½ cups pulp
¼ cup corn - lightly crushed in a pestle-mortar, 2-3 green onions - chopped, keep greens separate
1 tbsp Leonardo Olive Pomace Oil, ½ tsp cumin (*jeera*), 1 tsp chopped ginger, 1 tsp chopped garlic
1 green chilli - chopped
salt, pepper to taste, 1 tomato - chopped, a few drops lemon juice

LOW CAL MAKHANI GRAVY

5 large (500 gms) tomatoes - each cut into 4 pieces, 1 green chilli - chopped
2 tbsp Leonardo Olive Pomace Oil, 1 tsp flour (*maida*), ½ tsp cumin seeds (*jeera*)
4-5 flakes garlic and ½" piece ginger - ground to a paste (1½ tsp ginger-garlic paste)
2 tbsp tomato puree, 1 tbsp dry fenugreek leaves (*kasoori methi*), 1 tsp tomato ketchup
2 tsp coriander (*dhania*) powder, ½ tsp garam masala
1¼ tsp salt, or to taste, ½ tsp red chilli powder (optional), 1 cup water, ½ cup milk, approx.

TOPPING

a few ginger juliennes and coriander leaves - dipped in water

1. Sprinkle paneer with red chilli, salt & chaat masala. Rub masala to coat both sides. Keep aside.
2. For the makhani gravy, boil tomatoes with green chilli in ½ cup water. Simmer for 4-5 minutes on low heat till tomatoes turn soft. Remove from heat and cool. Grind the tomatoes along with the water to a smooth puree. Strain puree.
3. Heat Leonardo Olive Pomace Oil in a kadhai. Reduce heat. Add cumin. When it turns golden, add ginger-garlic paste. When paste starts to change colour add prepared tomato puree and cook till dry. Sprinkle flour and stir for 2 minutes till well blended. Add ready made tomato puree, dry fenugreek leaves and tomato ketchup. Reduce heat. Add masalas - coriander powder, garam masala, salt and red chilli powder. Mix well for a few seconds. Cook till Leonardo Olive Pomace Oil separates. Add water. Boil. Simmer on low heat for 4-5 minutes. Reduce heat. Keep aside to cool. Add enough milk to the cold masala to get a thick curry, mix gently. (Remember to add milk only after the masala cools, to prevent curdling). Keep aside.
4. For filling, heat 1 tbsp Leonardo Olive Pomace Oil. Add cumin and let it turn golden. Add ginger, garlic and green chilli. Stir. Add white of green onions and stir till golden. Add mashed brinjals and saute for 3-4 minutes. Add salt, pepper and red chilli powder. Add corn and stir. Add tomatoes and greens of onions. Add lemon juice. Keep filling aside.
5. Pan fry paneer slices till golden on both sides.
6. Place some filling on a layer of paneer. Cover with another slice and repeat filling. Place the final slice of paneer. Press well. Put some gravy in a square/rectangle dish. Place the manzil-e-paneer on it. Cover with gravy. Garnish with ginger juliennes & coriander. Microwave for 1½-2 minutes to serve.

LEONARDO
Olive Pomace Oil

Gatte ki Kadhi

Kadhi is a thick liquid made by blending gram flour with yogurt and simmering it gently. Dumplings or vegetables can be added, but here you find the addition of gatte, spongy cubes made from a well-spiced gram flour dough.

Serves 4

GATTE

1½ cups gram flour (*besan*)
1 tbsp yogurt (*dahi*)
a pinch of baking soda (*mitha soda*), ¾ tsp carom seeds (*ajwain*)
¾ tsp coriander seeds (*saboot dhania*), 1 tsp pomegranate (*anardana*)
2 tbsp Leonardo Olive Pomace Oil
1 green chilli - finely chopped, 1 tbsp green coriander - finely chopped
8-10 mint leaves - finely chopped
1 tsp salt, or to taste

KADHI

2 cups yogurt
2 tbsp gram flour (*besan*), 1 tsp cumin seeds (*jeera*)
1 tsp mustard seeds (*rai* or *sarson*), ½ tsp fennel (*saunf*)
a pinch of asafoetida (*hing*)
1 tsp turmeric (*haldi*) powder, 2 tsp red chilli powder
1 tsp coriander (*dhania*) powder, salt to taste
2 tbsp Leonardo Olive Pomace Oil
2 tbsp finely chopped fresh coriander

1. Mix all the ingredients for gatte together and knead a firm dough using about 4-5 tbsp water Shape dough into cylinders with greased hands as the dough is quite sticky.
2. Boil gatte in water for 10-12 minutes till they turn slightly yellowish white.
3. Keep these aside and cut them into 1″ pieces.
4. For the kadhi, mix yogurt & gram flour together, add turmeric powder & salt & mix well.
5. Heat Leonardo Olive Pomace Oil in a *kadhai*, add asafoetida, cumin seeds and mustard seeds, when they start spluttering add fennel. Wait till it changes colour.
6. Add yogurt-gram flour mixture. Add 4-5 cups of water. Bring to a boil, add red chilli powder and coriander powder and the gatte, cook the kadhi on low heat for 20-25 minutes. Serve with rice/roti.

Bhuna Gosht

'Gosht' mean 'meat' and 'bhuna' means 'stir-fried'. But this is stir-frying with a difference! The ingredients are stirred in Leonardo Olive Pomace Oil on low heat till their water content is reduced, they begin to brown, and the Leonardo Olive Pomace Oil shows at the sides of the pan. This method allows the meat to fully absorb all the aromas and flavours of the spices and become beautifully tender and well browned.

Serves 4

½ kg mutton with bones (from leg or shoulder) - cut into 1½" pieces
1" cinnamon stick (*dalchini*)
2 green cardamoms (*chhoti elaichi*)
2 onions - thinly sliced
1 tsp ginger paste
2 tsp garlic paste
½ tsp turmeric (*haldi*) powder
1 tsp red chilli powder
6 tbsp Leonardo Olive Pomace Oil
1 tsp salt

1. Heat Leonardo Olive Pomace Oil in a pressure cooker. Add the cinnamon stick and cardamoms. Wait for a minute. Add the onions and fry for 8-10 minutes on medium heat till golden brown.
2. Add ginger and garlic paste and stir for 1-2 minutes. Add salt, turmeric powder, chilli powder and meat pieces. Fry on medium flame stirring constantly for 5-7 minutes till the mutton turns glossy and has a well fried look.
3. Add ¾ cup water, give 1 whistle and simmer for 10 minutes. Remove from heat and let the pressure drop by itself.
4. Remove lid and check meat for doneness. Dry away any excess water on heat till Leonardo Olive Pomace Oil floats on the surface of mutton. Serve hot.

Jhatpat Vegetable Korma

This classic curry has the perfume of cardamom, cloves and cinnamon. The smooth rich gravy is made with a paste of onions, milk, coconut milk and cream. Paneer cubes and multi- coloured vegetables glow in this party dish.

Serves 4

4 baby corns - cut into thick slices, 6 small florets of cauliflower
5-6 French beans - chopped
1 carrot - diced into ½" pieces
75 gms paneer - cut into ½" pieces
1½ tbsp Leonardo Olive Pomace Oil, 4 cloves (*laung*), 1" piece cinnamon (*dalchini*)
2 green cardamoms (*chhoti elaichi*), ½ tsp cumin seeds (*jeera*)
3 onions - ground to a paste, 2 tsp ginger-garlic-green chilli paste
1 tsp salt, ½ tsp garam masala, ¼ tsp chilli powder, ¼ tsp pepper
½ cup milk, ½ cup coconut milk, 2 tbsp cream

1. Heat Leonardo Olive Pomace Oil, add cloves, cinnamon, cardamoms and cumin seeds. When cumin seeds crackle, add the onion paste and cook till onions turn light golden. Add the ginger-garlic-green chilli paste and cook for a minute. Sprinkle a tbsp water and stir for ½ minute.
2. Add carrot, beans, cauliflower and baby corns. Mix well. Stir for 2-3 minutes. Add salt, garam masala, chilli powder and pepper. Stir to mix well. Add ¼ cup water. Cover and cook on low heat till the vegetables are soft.
3. Add milk, coconut milk, cream and paneer. Cook on low heat for 1-2 minutes. Garnish with coriander leaves and serve hot.

Maharashtrian Toor Dal

A touch of sweet and sour ((jaggery and lemon) gives this delicious dal the distinctive touch of the food of Maharashtra.

Serves 2-3

½ cup pigeon pea split (*toor dal*)
¾ tsp salt, or to taste
½ tsp turmeric (*haldi*) powder
1 tbsp jaggery (*gur*)
1 tbsp lemon juice, or to taste

TADKA/TEMPERING

2 tbsp Leonardo Olive Pomace Oil
a pinch of asafoetida (*hing*)
½ tsp mustard seeds (*rai*)
some curry leaves

1. Clean, wash dal. Soak dal in 1½ cups of water for half an hour. Drain.
2. Pressure cook dal with 2 cups water, salt and turmeric on high flame till the first whistle and then simmer for 5 minutes. Remove from heat.
3. After the pressure drops, add jaggery and ½ cup water. Mix well. Simmer for 2-3 minutes. Remove from heat. The consistency should be thick.
4. For tadka/tempering heat Leonardo Olive Pomace Oil, add asafoetida and mustard seeds. Let it crackle and add curry leaves and immediately add it to the dal. Squeeze lemon juice on it. Check taste. Serve with rice.

Butter Chicken

There is no 'butter' in this dish, just healthy Leonardo Olive Pomace Oil. The rich tomato gravy is made in 2 steps: (a) The tomatoes are boiled with ginger, garlic and spices and strained to make a puree.(b) The puree is cooked with the curry, rich with cream and cashew paste. Marinated, sautéed chicken pieces are then simmered in this velvety classic gravy.

Serves 4

MARINATE TOGETHER

1 medium sized chicken (800 gms) - cut into 12 pieces, few drops of orange red colour

½ cup yogurt - hang for 45 minutes in a muslin cloth, 1 tbsp garlic paste

1 tbsp dry fenugreek leaves (*kasoori methi*), ½ tsp black salt, 1 tsp garam masala, ½ tsp salt

MAKHANI GRAVY

<u>Boil Together</u>

½ kg (6-7) tomatoes - roughly chopped

½" piece of ginger and 10 flakes of garlic - finely chopped

2 green chillies - chopped, 5-6 cloves (*laung*)

4-5 green cardamoms - pounded to open

1½ tsp Kashmiri laal mirch or *degi mirch*, 2 cups water

<u>Add later to the gravy</u>

2 tbsp Leonardo Olive Pomace Oil, 1 tsp ginger-garlic paste, 1 tsp kashmiri red chilli (*degi mirch*) powder

4 tbsp cashewnuts (*kaju*) - soak in ¼ cup hot water for 15 minutes, grind to a smooth paste

2 tbsp Leonardo Olive Pomace Oil, ¼ cup cream, ½ tsp garam masala, 1 tsp salt, or to taste

2 tsp tandoori masala (optional), ¼ tsp sugar or to taste

1 tbsp dry fenugreek leaves (*kasoori methi*) - dry roasted on a *tawa* for 2 minutes & crushed to a powder

1. Wash the chicken well. Pat dry chicken with a clean kitchen napkin. For the marinade, mix hung yogurt, garlic paste, dry fenugreek leaves, black salt, garam masala and colour. Rub the chicken with this mixture. Keep aside for 30 minutes or preferably overnight in the fridge.
2. Heat 6 tbsp Leonardo Olive Pomace Oil in a kadhai, add marinated chicken, cook on high heat for 5-6 minutes, stirring all the time. Reduce heat and cook covered for 7-8 minutes or till tender. Remove from heat. Keep aside.
3. To prepare the makhani gravy, boil tomatoes with all the ingredients. Reduce heat and cook covered on low heat for 15 minutes till slightly reduced in quantity. Remove from heat and transfer to a big flat utensil like a *paraat*. Cool completely for 15 minutes. Grind to a smooth puree. Strain puree through a metal strainer.
4. Heat 2 tbsp Leonardo Olive Pomace Oil in a kadhai. Add 1 tsp ginger-garlic paste and stir till golden. Add 1 tsp degi mirch. Stir and add prepared tomato puree. Boil. Cook for 5-7 minutes. Add all the remaining ingredients of the gravy. Bring to a boil, stirring continuously. Cook on medium heat till you get the desired colour and thickness of the gravy. Add a pinch of colour if needed.
5. Add cooked chicken. Simmer for 2 minutes till the gravy turns to a bright colour. Garnish with 1 tbsp of fresh cream and slit green chillies. Serve hot.

Hyderabadi Shahi Machhi Korma

Fish pieces are lightly fried till golden, then added to the korma at the very end. True to its Hyderabadi heritage, this korma is enriched with yogurt, poppy seeds, almonds, saffron and garam masalas, and is garnished with sliced boiled eggs.

Serves 2-3

250 gms firm boneless fish - cut into 1″ pieces
2 boiled eggs - halved
4 tbsp Leonardo Olive Pomace Oil
1 cup yoghurt (*dahi*) - whisked till smooth, ¼ tsp turmeric powder (*haldi*)
1¼ cups hot water, ½ tsp salt or to taste
a pinch of saffron (*kesar*) - crushed and soaked in 2 tbsp hot milk
2 tsp finely chopped fresh coriander

GRIND TO A FINE PASTE

2 dry, red chillies preferably Kashmiri - deseeded and soaked in water for 15 minutes
2 tsp poppy seeds (*khus-khus*) - soaked in 4 tbsp hot water for 15 minutes
1 tbsp almond - boil in water for 2 minutes
2 onions - chopped, 2 tbsp ginger-garlic paste, 1 green chilli - chopped
½ tsp black peppercorns (*saboot kali mirch*), 2 tsp coriander seeds (*saboot dhania*)
1 tsp cumin seeds (*jeera*), ½ tsp turmeric (*haldi*), 1 tsp garam masala, 1 tbsp lemon juice

1. Rub the washed fish pieces with ¼ tsp salt and a pinch of turmeric powder. Keep aside for 5 minutes.
2. Heat 2 tbsp Leonardo Olive Pomace Oil in a heavy-bottomed pan. Add fish pieces and gently fry until they are light golden in color. Remove fish pieces from the pan and drain them on absorbent paper.
3. Drain the red chillies. Peel almonds and chop roughly. Grind chillies and almonds with all the other ingredients of the paste.
4. Heat 2 more tbsp of Leonardo Olive Pomace Oil in the same pan. Add the ground paste and stir fry on medium heat for 5 minutes.
5. Reduce heat. Add yoghurt stirring continuously with the other hand. Keep stirring for about 4 minutes.
6. Add 1¼ cups hot water and bring to a boil.
7. Add salt. Mix.
8. Add the fish pieces. Stir gently. Cover and cook on low heat for about 5 minutes.
9. Gently stir in the saffron milk and sprinkle the fresh coriander.
10. To serve add the sliced boiled eggs. Serve hot with steamed rice or roti.

Appam with Vegetable Stew

Appams from Kerala are light and airy pancakes, white on top and golden underneath. The process of making them starts by soaking rice and urad dal, then grinding it to a coarse paste with coconut water and allowing it to ferment overnight. Learn to make them perfectly every time in these step-by-step instructions. Serve them with Vegetable Stew.

Makes 6

1 cup raw rice, permal rice, ¼ cup urad dal
1 cup coconut water, cocoa jal
½ tsp salt, ½ tsp sugar
½ tsp baking soda (*mitha soda*)
½ cup coconut milk
¾ tsp eno fruit salt, optional
Leonardo Olive Pomace Oil for greasing
6″ appam wok or a small non stick pan

1. Clean, wash and soak the rice and urad dal for 3 hours. Grind to a paste (not very fine), adding coconut water as required to get a thick pouring consistency. Add salt, sugar and baking soda, stir well. Cover and keep overnight to ferment. Do not put it in a cupboard or a warm place for fermentation.
2. At serving time, add coconut milk to the batter to get a thin pouring consistency which coats the back of a laddle (*kaddchi*). If needed add ¼-1/3 cup water to thin down the batter.
3. Heat a small nonstick fry pan or an appam kadhai (*chatti*) and brush with a little Leonardo Olive Pomace Oil.
4. Add eno fruit salt to the batter and mix well. Remove *chatti* from heat. Add about ¾ ladleful of the batter in the centre of the kadhai and swirl immediately taking it upto the sides nicely. Do not spread the batter with the *kaddchi*, else all the holes will get blocked.
5. Cover and cook over low heat for 2-3 minutes. The edges should be thin and crisp, while the centre soft and spongy. The top is whitish but the underside is light golden. Serve.

LEONARDO
Olive Pomace Oil
For Indian Cuisine and Frying

Vegetable Stew

Serve this mild Kerala curry in small katoris as it is quite thin, and serve appams to go with it. A variety of fresh vegetables are cut in neat pieces and simmered in a light, fragrant sauce which gets a touch of sweetness from coconut milk.

Makes 4

1 carrot - cut into small cubes
10 french beans - cut into ½" pieces, ½ cup shelled peas
1 small potato - cut into small cubes
½ cup small florets of cauliflower or broccoli, optional
2 sprigs curry leaves, 3-4 green chillies - slit
2 medium size onions - chopped
1 tsp ginger paste, 1 tsp garlic paste
1¼ tsp salt, or to taste
½-1 tsp chilli powder, optional
2½ cups coconut milk
1½ tbsp cornflour
2 tbsp chopped coriander, ½ tsp garam masala, ¼ tsp crushed pepper

TEMPERING

2 tbsp Leonardo Olive Pomace Oil
2 bay leaves (*tej patta*), ½ tsp mustard seeds (*sarson*), 4 cloves (*laung*)
2 cinnamon pieces, about 1" cinnamon (*dalchini*)
3 black cardamoms (*moti elaichi*)
½ tsp pepper corns (*saboot kali mirch*)

1. Heat Leonardo Olive Pomace Oil, add all ingredients of tempering and wait till fragrant, about a minute.
2. Add curry leaves, slit chillies and onions. Saute onions lightly till translucent and start to change colour, do not allow them to get brown.
3. Add ginger-garlic pastes, fry for a minute.
4. Add vegetables, stir fry for a while. When they get slightly soft about 3-4 minutes, add salt, chilli powder and ½ cup coconut milk mixed with ½ cup water and 1 tbsp cornflour. Cover and cook on low heat till the vegetables are done and the liquid has almost dried up.
5. Add the remaining coconut milk, chopped coriander, garam masala and crushed pepper. If it appears thick, add about ½ cup hot water. Boil for 2-3 minutes. Remove from heat. Check salt and masalas. Serve with appam.

Note: You can blanch or steam the vegetables if you like before cooking.

Dum Aloo Chutney Wale

A freshly made chutney of mint and coriander leaves and tart raw mangoes gives a lively lift to a white yogurt-cashew curry in which fried potato cubes are simmered. A delicate balance that gives pure joy.

Serves 2-3

2 potatoes - each cut into 4 cubes or 10-12 baby potatoes - keep whole

HARI CHUTNEY (GRIND TOGETHER)

1 cup chopped fresh coriander, ½ small raw mango or ½ tsp dry mango (*amchoor*) powder

½ cup mint (*poodina*), ½ tsp salt, ½ tsp sugar

GRAVY

4 tbsp Leonardo Olive Pomace Oil

1 tsp cumin (*jeera*) seeds, 2 onions - ground to a paste

4 tsp ginger-garlic paste, 1 tsp red chilli powder

1 cup yoghurt and 2 tbsp cashewnuts (*kaju*) - ground to a paste till smooth

1 cup water, 1 tsp salt, or to taste, 1 tomato - chopped finely, ½ tsp garam masala

1. Peel and wash potatoes. Cut into cubes. Heat Leonardo Olive Pomace Oil in a *kadhai* and deep fry over low heat until cooked and light brown.
2. For gravy, grind cashews and yoghurt to a smooth paste. Heat Leonardo Olive Pomace Oil in a kadhai. Add cumin, wait for a minute till golden. Add onion paste, stir over low heat until transparent. Do not brown the onions.
3. Add the ginger-garlic paste and stir until the masala leaves Leonardo Olive Pomace Oil. Add yoghurt and cashews paste. Stir for 1-2 minutes. Add hari chutney and red chilli powder. Stir till Leonardo Olive Pomace Oil separates and the mixture turns dry.
4. Add 1 cup water, stirring continuously on low heat till it comes to a boil.
5. Now add the fried potatoes and salt. Simmer uncovered for 5 minutes until the Leonardo Olive Pomace Oil leaves the masala and the gravy turns thick.
6. Add chopped tomato and garam masala, stir and bring to a boil. Serve.

Note: Do not cover the kadhai while cooking, as yogurt or milk based gravies can curdle if covered while cooking.

Rice & Roti

Missi Mirchi Parantha

Sometimes a plain parantha is not enough to satisfy your craving so try this variation – spread a paste of gram flour between multiple layers that are shaped into a spiral lachha parantha – learn the method with these clear instructions.

Makes 4

regular kneaded dough for 4 paranthas

4 tsp Leonardo Olive Pomace Oil for frying

FILLING

7 tbsp gram flour (*besan*), 4 tbsp Leonardo Olive Pomace Oil, ½-¾ tsp salt (depending on if the dough has salt or not)

1 tsp red chilli powder, ½ tsp carom seeds (*ajwain*)

1. Mix gramflour with Leonardo Olive Pomace Oil in a small bowl to get a thick paste of spreading consistency. Add salt, red chilli and spices. Keep aside.
2. Make 4 balls from the dough. Roll out each ball to a circle of 6″ diameter. Spread some gram flour paste, about 1½ tbsp, all over.
3. Roll into a long strip. Roll the strip to get a flattened ball. Press ball and tuck the end by pressing nicely beneath. Press from top gently. Roll out, applying very little pressure, to form the lachha parantha. If too much pressure is applied, the layers stick to each other and do not open up later.
4. Put on a hot tawa. Reduce heat. When the underside gets done, before turning the parantha, quickly put a tsp of Leonardo Olive Pomace Oil in the centre and turn the parantha immediately. (Do not spread Leonardo Olive Pomace Oil). When it gets fried, fry the other side by turning the parantha, but no Leonardo Olive Pomace Oil is required the second time. Once done, remove to a cloth napkin and serve lightly crushed to open the layers.

Palak Paneer Parantha

The parantha dough has onion seeds (kalonji) and the filling, made from mashed paneer and spinach, has carom seeds (ajwain). As soon as the parantha is ready it is brushed with milk and cooked again – irresistibly delicious!

Makes 4

DOUGH

1 cup whole wheat flour (*atta*), 1 tbsp Leonardo Olive Pomace Oil ¼ tsp onion seeds (*kalaunji*)

FILLING

2 tbsp Leonardo Olive Pomace Oil

250 gms spinach (*palak*) - leaves finely chopped (2 cups)

¼ tsp carom seeds (*ajwain*), 1 tsp ginger, garlic, ¼ tsp finely chopped chilli paste

50 gms paneer - mashed

¼ tsp salt or to taste, 1/8 tsp red chilli powder

¼ tsp dry mango powder (*amchoor*)

2-3 tbsp Leonardo Olive Pomace Oil for frying

1. Mix flour, Leonardo Olive Pomace Oil and onion seeds with enough water to get a soft dough of rolling consistency. Keep aside covered.
2. Heat 2 tbsp Leonardo Olive Pomace Oil. Add carom seeds and wait till light golden. Add ginger, garlic and chopped chilli, saute for 1-2 minutes. Add chopped spinach and cook till dry on medium flame. Add salt, red chilli powder, dry mango powder and grated paneer cook for 2-3 minutes till dry. Remove from pan and keep aside to cool.
3. To make the paranthas, divide the dough into 4 balls. Roll out each ball into a small circle. Place the filling in the center and collect from all sides to enclose the filling. Press over dry flour and roll into medium sized paranthas. Heat a tawa. Cook parantha on both sides on medium heat. Spread some Leonardo Olive Pomace Oil on both sides and cook till crisp. Serve hot.

Daal Biryani

In this pressure cooker recipe, the green moong dal is partially cooked with onions, herbs and spices, then rice is added and cooking continues till the rice is done. Mint leaves and lemon juice add a lovely freshness.

Makes 2-3

1 cup rice
½ cup green daal (*saboot moong dal*)
3 tbsp Leonardo Olive Pomace Oil
1 tsp cumin seeds (*jeera*)
1 onion - cut into slices
2" piece ginger - chopped finely
2 green chillies - chopped finely
6-8 peppercorns (*saboot kali mirch*) - crushed
2 tbsp tomato puree
½ tsp garam masala
½ tsp red chilli powder
2 tbsp chopped mint or coriander
salt to taste
juice of ½ lemon

1. Soak rice and keep aside. Heat 3 tbsp Leonardo Olive Pomace Oil in a pressure cooker. Add cumin seeds.
2. When cumin seeds turns golden, add onions, ginger, green chillies and peppercorns.
3. Stir till onions turn light brown. Reduce heat. Add tomato puree.
4. Cook for 1 minute on low heat. Add washed dal, ¾ tsp salt, garam masala, red chilli powder and 2½ cups water. Mix well. Pressure cook to give 1 whistle. Release pressure by putting cooker under running water.
5. Open the lid. Add the rice, coriander or mint, ¾ tsp salt and lemon juice. Pressure cook to give 1 whistle. Keep it on low heat for 1 minute. Remove from heat. Keep aside till pressure drops. Serve with tomato-onion raita.

Soya and Pea Pilaf

This traditional Rice and Peas Pilaf has all the typical spices including whole garam masalas. However, there is an added ingredient, soya granules, which gives extra nutritional value. The soya granules must be soaked in hot water before they can be used.

Serves 4

1 cup rice
½ cup soya granules
1 cup shelled green peas
4 tbsp Leonardo Olive Pomace Oil
1 onion - chopped fine
1 tsp ginger paste, 1 tsp garlic paste
2 black cardamoms (*moti elaichi*)
2-3 cloves (*laung*)
1" stick cinnamon (*dalchini*)
1 bay leaf (*tej patta*)
2 tsp salt or to taste
1 tsp garam masala powder
2 tbsp raisins (*kishmish*) - soaked in water and drained

1. Boil soya granules in water for 5 minutes. Keep aside in hot water.
2. Heat 4 tbsp Leonardo Olive Pomace Oil. Add onions, cinnamon, bay leaves, cloves and black cardamoms. Fry till onions turn brown.
3. Add ginger and garlic paste. Fry for 1 minute.
4. Drain soya. Add drained soya granules and peas to browned onions. Add garam masala. Fry for 3-4 minutes.
5. Add washed rice. Fry for 1 minute. Add raisins. Mix.
6. Add 2 cups water and salt. Boil.
7. Lower heat & cover. Cook for 12-15 minutes till all the water is absorbed & rice is cooked.

Tamarind Rice

Cooked rice is mixed with a thick, tangy tamarind chutney loaded with a range of tingling and tempting spices and nuts – a unique and exciting taste!

Serves 4

1 cup rice - boiled in 6-7 cups water with 1 tsp salt and drained
1-2 tbps Leonardo Olive Pomace Oil to sprinkle
1 walnut size ball tamarind
½ cup grated copra
¼ cup + 1 tbsp Leonardo Olive Pomace Oil
1 tsp mustard seeds
2 pinches asafoetida (*hing*)
2 red chillies
¾ tsp salt to taste
½ tsp turmeric powder
1 tbsp bengal gram dal (*channa dal*)
1 tbsp black gram dal (*urad dal*)
2 sprigs curry leaves
¼ cup roasted ground nuts

DRY ROAST AND POWDER

1 tsp coriander seeds (*saboot dhania*)
½ tsp fenugreek seeds (*methi dana*)
½ tsp pepper corns (*saboot kali mirch*)
½ tsp cumin seeds (*jeera*)
¼ cup peanuts, ½ cup sesame seeds (*til*)

1. Boil rice. Spread the cooked rice on a plate, sprinkle some Leonardo Olive Pomace Oil and toss with a fork, cover lightly and keep aside.
2. Boil tamarind in water, take out thick extract, about ½ cup pulp. Strain, keep aside.
3. Heat ¼ cup Leonardo Olive Pomace Oil, add ½ tsp mustard, a pinch of asafoetida, red chillies (broken into 2-3 pieces each). When mustard splutters, add tamarind water, salt and simmer on low heat till a thick chutney consistency is formed.
4. Heat 1 tbsp Leonardo Olive Pomace Oil in a kadhai, add ½ tsp mustard, a pinch of asafoetida. When done, add bengal gram dal, black gram dal and curry leaves.
5. When dals turn brown, add the tamarind chutney, turmeric and freshly prepared powders. Add grated copra and simmer 3-5 minutes. When Leonardo Olive Pomace Oil surfaces, add ground nuts. Mix.
6. Add rice and mix well for 1-2 minutes.

Murg Pulao

Well-marinated chicken pieces are sautéed in a pan; rice and water are added, and the biryani is all set to cook on low heat. The main flavor comes from the marinade which has onions, garlic, ginger, garam masalas and fennel seeds, but since it also has turmeric the rice gets an appetizing soft yellow colour.

Makes 2

1 cup basmati rice - washed & soaked in 2 cups water for 30 minutes
250 gms chicken - cut into pieces
1 tsp salt, 3 tbsp Leonardo Olive Pomace Oil

PASTE

3 dry, red chillies - deseeded, 2 onions - chopped,1 tbsp Leonardo Olive Pomace Oil
½ tsp salt, ¼ tsp turmeric (*haldi*) powder, 12-14 flakes garlic - chopped
2 tsp chopped ginger, 1 tbsp cumin seeds (*jeera*), 2 tsp fennel (*saunf*)
1" stick cinnamon (*dalchini*), seeds of 2 black cardamoms (*moti elaichi*), 3 cloves (*laung*)
8 peppercorns (*saboot kali mirch*)

1. Soak rice in 2 cups water for 30 minutes.
2. For the paste grind all ingredients together, using some water.
3. Mix chicken and the prepared paste. Marinate for 2-3 hours.
4. Heat 3 tbsp Leonardo Olive Pomace Oil. Add the chicken with the marinade and stir fry for 3-4 minutes till it changes colour.
5. Add rice along with the water. Add 1 tsp salt. Mix. Cover & cook on low heat for 13 minutes.
6. Separate the grains with a fork. Serve hot.

Brown Coriander Rice

Fiber-rich unpolished brown rice is very healthy though a bit chewy, and it takes more water to cook. In this recipe the rice and the vegetables absorb the flavours of the coriander paste mixture.

Serves 4

1 cup brown rice - wash and soak for 15 minutes
200 gms spinach (*palak*) - chopped, washed & drained well (2 cups)
1 cup grated carrot, ½ cup corn, 1 large onion - sliced finely
1½ tsp salt
3 tbsp Leonardo Olive Pomace Oil

CORIANDER PASTE

½ cup chopped coriander, 1 tsp chopped ginger, 2 green chillies, 5-6 flakes garlic
2 green cardamoms (*chhoti elaichi*), 2 cloves (*laung*), 2 tbsp water to grind

1. Wash rice and keep aside.
2. Grind all the ingredients of the paste. Keep aside.
3. Heat Leonardo Olive Pomace Oil. Add onion. Cook till golden brown.
4. Add the coriander paste, cook for 2-3 minutes on low flame.
5. Add chopped spinach, corn and carrot. Stir on high flame till dry.
6. Add rice and 3 cups water. Add salt. Mix. Bring to a good boil.
7. Cover the pan of rice with a well fitting lid. Cook on very low heat for about 22-25 minutes till the rice is done and the water gets absorbed.

Desserts

Gulab Jamun with Milk Powder

Sometimes you are not able to get khoya for gulab jamuns – but in this recipe you won't need it! Make a dough from milk powder, flour, baking soda, cream and milk, shape into balls and fry them carefully till golden. Soak in sugar syrup that has been scented with cardamom – yes, it is as simple as that!

Serves 10

1 cup skimmed milk powder

2½ tbsp flour (*maida*)

¼ tsp baking soda (*mitha soda*), ¼ cup cream, 1 tsp milk or enough to knead the dough

Leonardo Olive Pomace Oil for deep frying

10-20 mitha dana (*prasaad goli*)

SUGAR SYRUP

2½ cups sugar, 3 cups water, ¼ tsp cardamom (*elaichi*) powder

1. For the sugar syrup, boil water and sugar. Keep boiling for 2 minutes on medium flame to get a sticky syrup but no thread. Add cardamom powder and keep aside to cool to room temperature. Gulab jamuns should not be put in hot syrup.
2. Put milk powder, flour and soda in a small *paraat* or flat plate. Add cream and mix well. Mix the mixture. If the dough appears hard, add 1 tsp milk and mix again.
3. Roll some dough carefully into a smooth round ball. If the ball has cracks, add a little more milk to the dough and mix lightly to a smooth dough.
4. Heat enough Leonardo Olive Pomace Oil in a kadhai on low heat to fry the gulab jamun. Leonardo Olive Pomace Oil should not be very hot.
5. To check if the mixture is ok, put a tiny ball in Leonardo Olive Pomace Oil. If it comes up without breaking, it is alright, otherwise if it breaks, you can add 1-2 tsp maida in the mixture and make balls again. If it turns brown immediately, remove Leonardo Olive Pomace Oil from heat and let it become less hot. Remove kadhai from heat after checking the ball.
6. Divide mixture into 10 parts. Roll each part to a nice round and stuff a mitha dana in each ball. Make all balls. Heat Leonardo Olive Pomace Oil again for frying. When slightly hot, slip balls carefully in the Leonardo Olive Pomace Oil. Keeping the heat very low, shake the kadhai with the help of a *sansi* or *pakad* very gently so as to turn the gulab jamuns without touching them and prevent them from sticking to the bottom. Once they turn golden you can use a slotted spoon to turn the gulab jamuns. Keep the flame so low that the gulab jamuns take about 5-6 minutes in Leonardo Olive Pomace Oil to turn to a dark brown colour. They should be in Leonardo Olive Pomace Oil for this long, otherwise they tend to remain uncooked from the centre.
7. Once the balls have turned dark brown take out from the Leonardo Olive Pomace Oil and put into the syrup which should be at room temperature.
8. Fry the remaining balls and keep all gulab jamuns to soak in the syrup for 2 hours.

Jalebi

The ingredients are few (flour, besan, yogurt, soda) but the technique has to be just right. If you did not succeed in earlier attempts to make jalebis, read the tips in this recipe and find out what went wrong. Now you will be able to produce hot, crisp, perfect jalebis every time!

Makes 1 kg

BATTER

1 cup flour (*maida*)

1¼-1½ cups homemade yogurt, preferably slightly sour like 1 day old yogurt

SUGAR SYRUP (SEE NOTE)

2 cups sugar, 1½ cups water, few strands of saffron (*kesar*)

OTHER INGREDIENTS

¼ tsp soda-bi-carb (*mitha soda*), 1 tbsp gramflour (*besan*)

Leonardo Olive Pomace Oil for deep frying

empty milk packet or a squeeze bottle

1. Mix flour and 1¼ cup yogurt to make a thick, soft dropping consistency batter like pokoda batter. Add ¼ cup more yogurt if the batter appears too thick. Keep this batter covered for 1-2 hours at room temperature for fermentation. In winter, the batter should be kept in a warm place or in the sun. Do not over-ferment the batter.
2. For the sugar syrup, heat sugar and water till sugar dissolves. Add saffron. Bring to a boil. Cook for 7-8 minutes on medium heat till you get a syrup of a slight sticky consistency. Do not cook longer to get a thread consistency. Keep aside to cool down to room temperature.
3. Take a flat bottom pan, a medium size non stick pan works well. Pour enough Leonardo Olive Pomace Oil for frying, about 1" height.
4. Add gramflour and soda to the batter. Mix well and spoon this batter in an empty milk packet or a squeeze bottle. If using a milk packet, after filling with batter, tie it with a rubber band and make a small cut at one corner of the packet. Thin jalebis will remain crisp for longer but very thin jalebis turn brown too fast.
5. Make jalebi shape directly into the medium hot Leonardo Olive Pomace Oil, piping from inside to outside and keeping a little distance between the rings. Pull the last ring towards the centre to lock the jalebi. Deep fry on medium heat for about 2-3 minutes, turning sides with tongs (*chimta*) till rich golden brown on both sides. First try one to check the thickness of your liking.
6. Take out the jalebi from the Leonardo Olive Pomace Oil and immediately dip into the sugar syrup at room temperature for ½ -1 minute. Serve hot.

Tip: Sugar syrup if over cooked will form a dry coating on the jalebi. If under-cooked, it will turn the jalebis soggy. So check the syrup between the thumb and fore finger. The sugar syrup should not be hot when the jalebis are put into it. The left over sugar syrup can be transferred to a bottle and kept in the refrigerator for 5-6 weeks.

Besan Laddoo

Gram flour, Leonardo Olive Pomace Oil and sugar – simple ingredients that are transformed in carefully controlled steps to make a complex little bomb of taste explosion.

Makes 15-20

2½ cups gram flour (*besan*), use coarsely ground
9 tbsp Leonardo Olive Pomace Oil
¼ tsp green cardamom powder (*chhoti elaichi*)
1 cup powdered sugar or *bura*

1. Heat Leonardo Olive Pomace Oil in a kadhai. Add the gram flour and keep stirring continuously over a medium flame for about 10 minutes till golden brown. Add the cardamom powder and mix well. Remove from heat and transfer to a *paraat*. If it remains in the kadhai it will become dark brown which should be avoided. Keep aside to cool in a *paraat* for 2-3 hours to cool completely or the laddoos will not hold shape and become flat.
2. After the gramflour is completely cool after 2-3 hours, mix powdered sugar and gram flour mixture together in a *paraat*. Rub with both hands for 3-4 minutes till well blended. Make laddoos.

Suji ka Halwa

If you have avoided suji halwa because it uses so much ghee – try this fantastic version which uses Leonardo Olive Pomace Oil instead! Suji halwa will once again be a regular feature at your table!

Serving 4

1 cup semolina (*suji*)
½ cup Leonardo Olive Pomace Oil
1 cup sugar
1 cup milk
3 cups water
seeds of 4 green cardamoms (*chhoti elaichi*) - crushed
few strands of saffron (*kesar*), 8-10 raisins (*kismish*)
8-10 almonds - cut into thin long pieces

1. Mix milk, water, crushed cardamoms, saffron and sugar.
2. Boil. Stir to dissolve the sugar. Keep aside.
3. Roast semolina in a pan on medium flame till fragrant. Do not let it turn brownish. This will take about 8-10 minutes.
4. Heat Leonardo Olive Pomace Oil in a kadhai. Fry semolina on low heat till it turns golden. Add raisins.
5. Add milk mixture, stirring continuously for 7-8 minutes till the halwa leaves the sides of the kadhai.
6. Remove from heat. Keep aside till serving time.
7. To serve, heat halwah and transfer to a serving dish. Decorate with shredded almonds and pista.

International Conversion Guide

These are not exact equivalents; they've been rounded-off to make measuring easier.

WEIGHTS & MEASURES

METRIC	IMPERIAL
15 g	½ oz
30 g	1 oz
60 g	2 oz
90 g	3 oz
125 g	4 oz (¼ lb)
155 g	5 oz
185 g	6 oz
220 g	7 oz
250 g	8 oz (½ lb)
280 g	9 oz
315 g	10 oz
345 g	11 oz
375 g	12 oz (¾ lb)
410 g	13 oz
440 g	14 oz
470 g	15 oz
500 g	16 oz (1 lb)
750 g	24 oz (1 ½ lb)
1 kg	30 oz (2 lb)

LIQUID MEASURES

METRIC	IMPERIAL
30 ml	1 fluid oz
60 ml	2 fluid oz
100 ml	3 fluid oz
125 ml	4 fluid oz
150 ml	5 fluid oz (¼ pint/1 gill)
190 ml	6 fluid oz
250 ml	8 fluid oz
300 ml	10 fluid oz (½ pint)
500 ml	16 fluid oz
600 ml	20 fluid oz (1 pint)
1000 ml	1¾ pints

CUPS & SPOON MEASURES

METRIC	IMPERIAL
1 ml	¼ tsp
2 ml	½ tsp
5 ml	1 tsp
15 ml	1 tbsp
60 ml	¼ cup
125 ml	½ cup
250 ml	1 cup

HELPFUL MEASURES

METRIC	IMPERIAL
3 mm	1/8 in
6 mm	¼ in
1 cm	½ in
2 cm	¾ in
2.5 cm	1 in
5 cm	2 in
6 cm	2½ in
8 cm	3 in
10 cm	4 in
13 cm	5 in
15 cm	6 in
18 cm	7 in
20 cm	8 in
23 cm	9 in
25 cm	10 in
28 cm	11 in
30 cm	12 in (1 ft)

HOW TO MEASURE

When using the graduated metric measuring cups, it is important to shake the dry ingredients loosely into the required cup. Do not tap the cup on the table, or pack the ingredients into the cup unless otherwise directed. Level top of cup with a knife. When using graduated metric measuring spoons, level top of spoon with a knife. When measuring liquids in the jug, place jug on a flat surface, check for accuracy at eye level.

OVEN TEMPERATURE

These oven temperatures are only a guide. Always check the manufacturer's manual.

	°C (*Celsius*)	°F (*Fahrenheit*)	Gas Mark
Very Low	120	250	1
Low	150	300	2
Moderately Low	160	325	3
Moderate	180	350	4
Moderately High	190	375	5
High	200	400	6
Very High	230	450	7

Herbs & Spices

Asafoetida
(Hing)

Bay Leaves
(Tej Patta)

Cardamom
(Chhoti Illaichi)

Cardamom, Black
(Moti Illaichi)

Carom Seeds
(Ajwain)

Green Chillies
(Hari Mirch)

Dry Red Chilli
(Sukhi Sabut Lal Mirch)

Red Chilli Powder
(Lal Mirch Powder)

Cinnamon
(Dalchini)

Cloves
(Laung)

Coriander Seeds
(Sabut Dhania)

Coriander Seeds Ground
(Dhania Powder)

Coriander Leaves
(Hara Dhania)

Cumin Seeds
(Jeera)

Black Cumin Seeds
(Shah Jeera)

Curry Leaves
(Kari Patta)

Fennel Seeds
(Saunf)

Fenugreek Seeds
(Methi Dana)

Fenugreek Leaves, Dried
(Kasuri Methi)

Garam Masala Powder
(Garam Masala)

Garlic
(Lahsun)

Ginger
(Adrak)

Mace
(Javitri)

Mango Powder, Dried
(Amchoor)

Melon Seeds
(Magaz)

Mint Leaves
(Pudina)

Black Mustard Seed
(Sarson)

Nigella, Onion Seeds
(Kalaunji)

Nutmeg
(Jaiphal)

Peppercorns
(Sabut Kali Mirch)

Pomegranate Seeds,
Dried (Anardana)

Sesame Seeds
(Til)

Saffron
(Kesar)

Turmeric Powder
(Haldi)

Brown Mustard Seed
(Rai)

Poppy Seeds
(Khus-Khus)

Nita Mehta's

INDIAN COOKING with OLIVE OIL

Snab Publishers Pvt Ltd

Corporate Office
3A/3, Asaf Ali Road, New Delhi 110 002
Phone: +91 11 2325 2948, 2325 0091
Telefax: +91 11 2325 0091
E-mail: nitamehta@nitamehta.com
Website: www.nitamehta.com

Editorial and Marketing office
E-159, Greater Kailash II, New Delhi 110 048

Food Styling and Photography by Snab
Typesetting by National Information Technology Academy
3A/3, Asaf Ali Road, New Delhi 110 002

Recipe Development & Testing:
Nita Mehta Foods - R & D Centre
3A/3, Asaf Ali Road, New Delhi - 110002
E-143, Amar Colony, Lajpat Nagar-IV, New Delhi - 110024

ISBN 978-81-7869-328-6
First Print 2011
Printed in India by IPP Ltd. Noida

Distributed by : NITA MEHTA BOOKS
NITA MEHTA BOOKS
3A/3, Asaf Ali Road, New Delhi - 02
Distribution Centre :
D16/1, Okhla Industrial Area, Phase-I,
New Delhi - 110020
Tel.: 26813199, 26813200
E-mail: nitamehta.mehta@gmail.com

Rs. 595/- US $ 24.95 UK £ 14.95